DØ827889

You Can't Have Him—
HE'S MINE

DISCARDED

A Woman's Guide to Affair-Proofing Her Relationship

MARIE H. BROWNE, R.N., PH.D., WITH MARLENE M. BROWNE, ESQ.

A

ADAMS MEDIA
AVON, MASSACHUSETTS

Published by
Adams Media, an F+W Publications Company
57 Littlefield Street, Avon, MA 02322. U.S.A.
www.adamsmedia.com

ISBN 10: 1-59869-121-X
ISBN 13: 978-1-59869-121-4

Printed in Canada.

J I H G F E D C B A

Library of Congress Cataloging-in-Publication Data
Browne, Marie H.
You can't have him—he's mine / Marie H. Browne with Marlene M. Browne.
p.   cm.
Includes bibliographical references.
ISBN-13: 978-1-59869-121-4 (pbk.)
ISBN-10: 1-59869-121-X (pbk.)
1. Marriage—Handbooks, manuals, etc. 2. Man-woman relationships—Hand-
books, manuals, etc. 3. Communication in marriage—Handbooks, manuals, etc.
4. Marriage—Psychological aspects. I. Browne, Marlene M. II. Title.
HQ734.B912 2007
646.7'8—dc22   2007001129

This publication is designed to provide accurate and authoritative information with
regard to the subject matter covered. It is sold with the understanding that the
publisher is not engaged in rendering legal, accounting, or other professional advice.
If legal advice or other expert assistance is required, the services of a competent
professional person should be sought.
     —From a *Declaration of Principles* jointly adopted by a Committee of the
American Bar Association and a Committee of Publishers and Associations

Many of the designations used by manufacturers and sellers to distinguish their
product are claimed as trademarks. Where those designations appear in this book
and Adams Media was aware of a trademark claim, the designations have been
printed with initial capital letters.

To protect the identity of my patients and to maintain their right to confidential
treatment, I've altered basic facts (names, ages, occupations, and geographical loca-
tions) presented in the case histories that follow; I have, however, faithfully pre-
served the essential elements that made these patient experiences illuminating and
instructive.—Marie H. Browne, R.N., Ph.D.

The nine-item list in Chapter 14 on page 223 is from "A Vision of Romantic Love"
by Nathaniel Branden, Ph.D., in *The Psychology of Love*, edited by R. J. Sternberg
and M. L. Barnes, Copyright © 1988. Used with permission of Yale University Press.
The Love Scale on page 225 is used with the permission of Dr. Alvin Pam. The Mate
Retention Inventory (MRI) on page 237 is adapted from *Personality and Individual
Differences*, Vol. 39, Shackelford, T. K., Goetz, A. T. & Buss, D. M., "Mate Retention in Marriage: Further Evidence of the Reliability of the Mate Retention Inventory," pp. 415–425, Copyright © 2005, with permission from Elsevier.

This book is available at quantity discounts for bulk purchases.
For information, please call 1-800-289-0963.

"There is nothing nobler or more admirable than when two people who see eye to eye keep house as man and wife, confounding their enemies and delighting their friends."

—Homer (800 B.C.E.)

Dedication

This book is for my deceased parents, who showed me the way; to my husband, who has been in my life since childhood, and throughout our long journey, we still laugh and enjoy each other's company; and to my daughter and son-in-law, who make my dark days bright. Finally, this book is for my patients, whose lives and experiences made this endeavor possible.

Contents

Part 3
Seizing Your Wifely Power / 115

Introduction

The statistics on infidelity are alarming. According to an article from the *Journal of Couple & Relationship Therapy* entitled "Cybersex: The New Affair Treatment Considerations," it is estimated that between 15 and 60 percent of husbands are cheating on their wives. If your husband is among them, you stand to lose not only your spouse, but also your psychic sense of trust, certainty, and the security of family life as you know it.

But there's good news. Many recent studies reveal that very happy marriages are far less vulnerable to infidelity than unhappy ones, and that extremely happy marriages are even more secure from the threat of adultery. The close association between marital satisfaction and fidelity is critical because so many popular self-help books written about adultery to date are premised on now-dated studies (based upon small sample sizes, questionable self-reporting methods, and retroactive accounts) that purported to find that even happy marriages are vulnerable to infidelity. If that were the case, you, the wife, would be a powerless victim of circumstance, having no control over your marital destiny. My many years of practice as a licensed marriage and family therapist lead me to disbelieve this claim.

To the contrary, I've witnessed how vigilant, vigorous, and skillfully administered mate-guarding tactics, not to mention psychological insight complemented with positive communication methods and conflict resolution skills, can work wonders to ward off the "other woman" who's on the scene—or waiting to pounce. As a registered nurse and a Ph.D., with more than forty years teaching psychology and thirty-five years treating couples whose marriages were nearly destroyed by a husband's infidelity as well as by the "other women" who formed the third part of the trauma triangle, I wrote this book—with the help of my daughter, a divorce lawyer—to share the accumulated wisdom of leading experts on love, marriage, mate-protection, forgiveness, and moving on, all punctuated with clinical examples from my practice.

With facts and theories from neuroscience, evolution, psychology, and sociology at your fingertips, you will gain the information, resources, and insight needed to decode what your husband is doing and why, while assessing the formerly inscrutable motives, approaches, and techniques of the other woman. Knowing what lies behind the impulse to steal another woman's mate allows you to recognize when a danger is present; predict what could happen if your husband is left unattended; and, most important, permit you to manage the situation by taking precise actions to eliminate the marital threat that you've discovered or that your husband has disclosed. As you'll see, a wife who knows what to look for and how to react can take control before real trouble starts, making her marriage resistant to the well-known stressors, circumstances, and noxious opportunities that arise in certain environments known to create fertile fields for extramarital interaction.

You'll become expert at assessing your mate and the quality of your marriage and home life for infidelity vulnerability. I'll help you explore your role in the marriage, as you obtain a realistic view of yourself as a mate and companion. You'll learn if your wifely actions could be construed as mate-guarding or oblivious, with attitudes and actions—conscious or unconscious—that make an affair all but inevitable. You'll learn strategies that can put you and your marriage back on a healthier track, even if an affair has already begun or has happened in the past. Remember, no matter who the other woman is, no matter what she does, it is possible to defeat her, so long as you are prepared, alert, and ready to act to protect what's yours.

Part 1

ASSESSING LOVE ON THE HOME FRONT

CHAPTER 1

Your Husband's Happiness Factor

As you'll learn throughout these pages, both commitment and relationship satisfaction can change over time, for better or worse. Everything changes; it's just a matter of how you deal with it. No one remains the same day after day, year after year. Relationships that deepen over time allow for the individuals in them to evolve and grow. Resisting the momentum of transformation will rarely have the desired effect of keeping circumstances static. Learning how to deal with life's inevitable changes and challenges—how you love and how you express your feelings—will help you and your spouse grow more intimate as years pass. And by the way, it never hurts to bear in mind the basics of human interaction. Most people respond to kindness and affirmation far better than they do to sarcasm and attack, and your spouse is probably no exception. (If he is, there are other problems, which you'll find discussed in later chapters.) Knowing that people like a positive approach over a negative one, learning to communicate in an affirmative, sincere, and loving way (think here, thoughtful and considerate) will be a theme running through this book and your relationship.

Moreover, minding the golden rule will help at nearly all points of human contact, certainly among your most intimate relationships. With one exception (addressed later), you want to treat your partner as you would like to be treated. The most successful relationships occur between two people who feel worthy of love, who trust that they can bring something to the relationship that is unique and special, and who believe that they deserve a mate who can do the same. Positive mutual enforcement in a relationship (knowing that you are worthy of love and care, and your mate is, too) promotes each partner's self-esteem and intensifies the satisfaction from the bond. (We enjoy being in the company of those who make us feel worthy, of value, and exceptional.) In fact, if your marital relationship lacks this affirmative aspect, look out. If negativity, contempt, and defensiveness reign in your relationship, your mate might be particularly vulnerable. Another woman might sense that a little attention or flattery is just what the doctor ordered and then proceed to dispense it to gain access to your man's inner sanctum, and eventually heart.

So much in your relationship rides on how and what you feel and perceive about each other, as individuals and as a couple. We'll explore what makes a mate happy and why, and what you—his partner—can or should be doing about it.

Scratching His Itch

At the most basic level, your mate's overall satisfaction (and yours, as well) depends upon the fulfillment of primary needs. Researchers who study couples and marriages believe that your ability to take care of your partner is extremely high on the list. Other functions of love can seem focused on the self (does this person meet my needs, make me feel good, fulfill my expectations?). Caretaking, on the other hand, is about giving of oneself to a partner. You must exhibit an interest in meeting your mate's needs, protecting him, and assuaging any harm or discomfort he might experience.

While general care giving is important in an adult intimate relationship, intimacy is even more critical to promoting a loving and satisfying relationship. More than a quarter of a century ago, researchers found a distinct connection between marital intimacy and sexuality. No big surprise there. In fact, further work on the issue revealed that most people consider sex a crucial element of intimacy, though not the primary one. (Sex was listed third in importance, after closeness and self-disclosure.)

THE EIGHT ELEMENTS OF MARITAL INTIMACY, ACCORDING TO THE WARING INTIMACY QUESTIONNAIRE:

1. **Conflict resolution:** The way a couple resolves their disagreements and differences of opinion
2. **Affection:** The manner in which the couple expresses tenderness and the desire for closeness
3. **Cohesion:** Unity as a couple manifested by commitment to and value of the marriage
4. **Sexuality:** How partners communicate and satisfy their respective sexual urges within the marriage
5. **Identity:** The way each spouse feels about him/herself (self-esteem and self-confidence)
6. **Compatibility:** How well the partners are suited to share time together, whether at work, play, or rest
7. **Autonomy:** The degree of independence the married couple has from offspring and other family
8. **Expressiveness:** How easily the spouses relate their values, goals, fears, opinion, beliefs, and feelings within the marriage

Though there are happily married couples who no longer have sex together, I can tell you from my nearly forty years in practice that they are not common. Moreover, if they are happy with a sexless union, there is usually a mutual reason for their arrangement: they are elderly, or they both accept that illness, medication, or injury affects performance and/or desire. The marriage might also be based upon one of the kinds of love that are not at all erotic or passionate. Instead, the partners accommodate each other for personal reasons and sexual union is not a part of their marriage pact. Whatever works for both spouses is fine, but when one spouse has a need that the other will not or can not meet, it's an invitation to trouble, particularly when someone else is ready to step into those shoes, or that bed, as the case may be. To avoid carnal vulnerability, let's look at what the social scientists have learned about marital sex and satisfaction.

Though sexual satisfaction generally ranks below overall intimacy in importance to married couples, the problem occurs as most men find their way to intimacy through sex, while most women require intimacy before sex. Yet a happy marriage with a satisfying sex life requires a mutual understanding, taking into account both partners' needs and desires.

Moreover, my clinical practice reveals that if a man's basic bodily needs for sex are not met, the marriage may become

Sex Is Good for Your Body and Your Relationship

According to researchers, sex not only promotes intimacy, it promotes your physical health. Sex has been shown to improve immune functioning, to decrease pain and insomnia, and to contribute towards feelings of well-being. But don't despair if you're not always in the mood. According to Dr. Legato, women "often don't have any desire for sex until they are physically in the act of lovemaking." So just do it, and reap all the benefits.

vulnerable to outside offers to provide what is missing in the marital bed. Many of these sorts of affairs begin as mere sexual flings, but biology can kick in, making the husband feel more closely connected to his sexual partner than to his spouse. This is a situation that any wife can avoid entirely by engaging in open communication about her sexual needs while taking into account her husband's, perhaps different, level of desire and interest in the physical aspect of their union.

Sexuality and Communication

When a couple is able to share their feelings about sex and discuss their physical appetites, most are able to reach an accommodation that will satisfy both partners. Contrary to what you might expect, spouses say that their sex lives are satisfying if they are compatible with their partners and committed to the relationship. Sexual satisfaction is generally not based upon whether a wife or husband performs a specific act. Rather, it depends upon a couple's mutual accommodation of each partner's desired physical range and frequency of contact. This accommodation, however, requires connection and open lines of communication.

In fact, just the act of addressing the topic of sex in conversation generally assuages the concerns of the couple. To discuss a subject is to explore it and work toward finding a solution. Couples that can converse about their sex lives have less to worry about from the threat of outside opportunities than those who refuse to (or cannot) discuss the subject, though both spouses know their sex life is not fulfilling for at least one of them. What do you do if you find discussing sexual topics taboo?

First survey the area. What is different now from when you were dating? Were you able to communicate about sex then? If not, think about what you can do to include sex in your list of marital discussion topics. Unless you are willing to share your feelings about your sex life, you will have to accept responsibility for contributing toward your situation. If you choose to remain mute on the subject of sex, your choice is for no change, no improvement. If, however, your marriage and your relationship with your husband are worth expanding your comfort zone to include discussing sex and sensuality, you will generally be rewarded by having a very grateful man as an audience, eager to make things better between you. Once you gain the courage or motivation to speak about sex, consider what makes it good: mutual respect, emotional safety, and acceptance of each other. Once you begin a dialogue, explore areas like these:

- Any difficulties with the physical aspects of sex
- Possible psychological obstacles and inhibitions to satisfying sex (religious or cultural beliefs or taboos, or gender/role fulfillment, to name a few)
- Pleasure and ability or inability to climax (perhaps you are too "goal oriented," losing sight of the sensual pleasure of loving touch for its own sake)
- Private or "forbidden" fantasies or fetishes
- Feelings of guilt or shame about past sexual experiences (like abuse) that might be affecting your present ability to enjoy a mutually satisfying sex life
- Interest in exploring positions, sensations, and toys, consider physical limitations in some cases
- Sharing respective sexual tastes and preferences (explicit turn-ons for your mate and for you)

If the problem isn't an inability to discuss the topic but a drop or cessation of sexual desire, consider your life circumstances. Are there young or ailing kids to care for? A demanding new job? Added stress from illness, parental dependency, or financial pressure? Do you harbor anger at other unresolved issues? Whatever the underlying reason for sexual disharmony between you and your husband, you have to address it and try to resolve the problem. If left untended, a persistently dissatisfying sexual relationship could poison your relationship, ultimately causing your mate to seek from others the sexual satisfaction he cannot find with you. Remember, your mate chose to be with you. Even if you have changed since your love was new, your man's need for your comfort, care, and physical companionship remains. Doubt it?

Consider the case of Alice and David. After spending nearly $100,000 and undergoing multiple in vitro fertilization procedures, Alice got pregnant and gave birth to the child the couple had desperately wanted. After the baby's birth, Alice was too tired to have sex. David understood and did not pressure her. He gave Alice time and space and help caring for their infant. He stayed quiet, hoping things between them would return to normal. Though he never told her expressly, sex was David's way of getting the love and reassurance he needed from his wife.

Months passed, the baby adopted a normal routine, and yet Alice still could not bring herself to have sex with her husband. She dreaded taking her clothes off and going to bed nude. Alice had gained nearly fifty pounds during her pregnancy and had

You Are Not Alone

A 1994 National Health and Social Life Survey found that the most common sexual problem for women was want of sexual desire (affecting approximately 33 percent) and inability to climax (24 percent). For the guys, ejaculating too soon was the number-one sexual problem (29 percent), while performance anxiety was number two (17 percent), and—get this—lack of sexual interest was a near tie (16 percent).

only lost ten of it after eight months. She felt fat, out of shape, and completely undesirable. She had always been fit and was not used to having the body of a brand-new mom. Until her pregnancy, she had known that her fabulous figure was a source of pride and sexual joy for her husband. Now, she felt nothing like that. What's more, after the vaginal delivery, she feared David wouldn't experience the same tightness he had before. Though she never articulated them, all these factors made Alice unable to have sex with David. Meanwhile, David grew sullen and withdrawn. He didn't complain about not having his wife available to make love with, but he was unhappy and didn't understand why she rejected him now that the baby was sleeping through the night.

I saw the couple in joint sessions to open the lines of communication. They could not have been more supportive of each other once they understood what was happening (David's continuing physical need for his wife and Alice's erroneous assumptions and false projections about her desirability to David). When Alice understood what David really thought and felt about her, she was able to accept her body for all that it had done for her, for them, and for their miracle baby. While she still hopes to lose the baby weight soon, until she does, she and her husband enjoy each other in every way. (For more on married sexuality, see Chapter 9.)

In addition to emotional closeness, caregiving, and sexuality, your man has other needs that you should know about and foster for a successful relationship, free from outside siren calls.

A Man's Maslow Needs

According to Abraham H. Maslow, "man is a perpetually wanting animal" and thus does not live by sex alone. If Maslow's theory of human motivation is correct (and though nearly impossible to test, many experts accept it), your husband has a hierarchy of drives (or needs), from the base to the transcendent, that he will try to fulfill over the course of his lifetime. Often represented as a triangle or a pyramid, Maslow's diagram of human needs places the basics (physiological needs) at the bottom, with each successive layer up the pyramid representing a higher level of developmental attainment.

For instance, the bottom tier of the triangle represents man's needs for physical and biological comforts like food, water, shelter, warmth, sex, and exercise. He cannot pursue the higher needs without first gratifying the human drive for physical balance. As Maslow stated in his 1943 paper, "A Theory of Human Motivation," for the dangerously hungry man, there is nothing but food on his mind: "He dreams food, he remembers food . . . he wants only food . . . Freedom, love, community feeling, respect, philosophy, may all be waved aside as fripperies which are useless since they fail to fill the stomach. Such a man may fairly be said to live by bread alone."

Maslow's Pyramid of Needs

Self-transcendence

Self-actualization

Appreciation of beauty/aesthetics

Pursuit of knowledge/experience

Self-esteem/ego needs

Love/belongingness needs

Safety/security needs

Physiological needs

The next level up on the pyramid's needs is safety (financial and physical security for self and family, or, as Norman Rockwell might have put it, "freedom from fear"). Above that is the need called "belongingness," attained by warm, affectionate relationships with lovers, friends, family, and a place in the community. Interestingly, Maslow distinguishes the sex need (the base, physiological drive) from the higher-level love need, characterized by the ability to give as well as receive devotion and tenderness, often expressed during the sex act between lovers. (This is where you want your lovemaking to be, as spouses.)

Once a person's need for love and belongingness are satisfied, he turns toward the drive for self-esteem, representing one's own, as well as the community's, recognition of one's achievement and competence in the world. All four bottom layers represent deficiency needs that must be met before a person can rise to the next level of human development.

After the deficiency needs are fulfilled, the next leap in development—signified by a gap in Maslow's hierarchy triangle—is for the growth or being needs to be satisfied. The first growth need is the pursuit of knowledge (the love of learning and acquiring experience and adventure). The next is appreciation of beauty, the aesthetic drive that elevates the soul to awe and wonder in the presence of the glorious and the magnificent, whether in nature or in a museum. After another gap, a man reaches for self-actualization, the penultimate step up the hierarchical pyramid. Self-actualization is characterized by realizing one's potential and becoming all that one can be. Self-actualized people are described as reality centered, solution focused, inner-directed, original, creative, and spontaneous. They have a sense of wonder, and though they enjoy solitude and autonomy, they have profound personal relations. They are accepting, ethical, and compassionate, with a good sense of values and of humor. The self-actualized are given to having "peak experiences," in which they are one with their work, experiencing a flow state that makes time melt and the performance, effortless. Maslow thought that only 2 percent of the world's population was self-actualized, a group that included Thomas Jefferson, Abraham Lincoln, Frederick Douglass, Albert Einstein, Eleanor Roosevelt, William James, Albert Schweitzer, and Aldous Huxley.

But there's more to life than self-actualization. Later in Maslow's career, he decided that transcendence was the pinnacle of motivational drives. The drive toward the spiritual represented the final frontier of a human's growth trajectory, in which a person finds meaning beyond himself that is eternal—even mystical—and that ultimately provides a sense of meaning for life in the world at large.

If you understand this constant upward pull of human development, you will see that you, as the spouse, are in a unique position to foster and support your husband's development. If you attempt to keep him stagnant—impeding his growth, rather than encouraging it—you are setting the stage for his existential discontent. Your partner's dissatisfaction will set him searching and seeking for ways, perhaps outside the marriage, to meet his developmental urges. (This is one of the reasons you hear divorced people explain that they and their spouses "grew apart." Often, this was really their failure to foster each other's mutual growth while keeping the marriage stable throughout those changes.)

Maslow's Definition	"A musician must make music, an artist must paint, a poet must write, if he is to be ultimately happy. What a man can be, he must be. This need we may call self-actualization." —Abraham Maslow (1908–1970)

The marital danger emanates from the pervasive, general unhappiness (manifested by melancholy, pessimism, despondency, antipathy, and worst of all for a marriage, estrangement) that results when a spouse's drive for development is stunted. I've seen this situation turn into the typical "Is this all there is?" complaint about life and marriage. To avoid this stage of unrest and dissatisfaction, a perceptive mate will do what she can to see his needs are met and that she too grows and continues to intrigue her man. If not, a discerning mate-seeker will sense a man's restiveness and try to key her actions to match his needs and interests. By coming to his developmental rescue, this would-be other woman will make your husband feel like his life has been leading up to meeting her, the midwife to his spiritual awakening. The key to avoiding this marital vulnerability is to share your husband's quest for meaning and, eventually, the more elusive goals of self-actualization and transcendence.

Consider my patient Jake, a technical wizard who made a good living as a computer specialist but who longed for something more. When I met him, he had been married for six years and had a child. He was nearing forty and feeling like his life was empty. Jake told me that he was a loyal man to his family but not to himself. He said he always wanted to go to law school and knew he was bright enough, but that his wife, Dawn, would not hear of it. The only one who encouraged him was a young lawyer, Lorrie, whom he had met at work. He said Lorrie understood his needs and they would talk for hours about history, politics, and the things he had always loved but had given up when he married Dawn. Though Dawn was a beauty, Jake felt now that they had nothing in common except their son, and that was not enough for him. Jake was looking forward to the summer, when Dawn would take up residence at the shore. Though he'd miss his son, Jake thought the arrangement would leave him more time for Lorrie during the workweek.

Though Jake made a point of mentioning how much more attractive Dawn was, he told me that he no longer cared about that. Lorrie had a nice body but also a beautiful mind, and now Jake needed a mate who would support his dreams, before it was too late. Jake wanted a companion who was interested in his happiness and see him as more than a paycheck. I suggested he share these feelings with his wife, allowing her the opportunity to respond and share her views and resolve the problem.

Jake reported that Dawn would not even entertain a discussion. At the same time, Lorrie had offered to give Jake a loan to pay for law school tuition, promising to tutor him as well. Lorrie had a plan. She was encouraging Jake's ambition, making him feel hopeful with a renewed sense of vitality. Dawn didn't realize what happened and didn't inquire, thankful that Jake seemed happier when he was around. When one of Dawn's friends saw Jake with Lorrie and reported it, Dawn thanked her and told her to mind her own business, replying that Jake would never leave her or their son.

Six months later, Jake told Dawn that he wanted a divorce and was in love with someone who understood him and cared about him. He planned to stop working and enter law school full time in the fall. He told Dawn she could have the house and all the contents and he would pay support from his savings as the law required. He would co-parent their son and suggested that Dawn look for employment since as they had been married less than ten years, he would not have to pay her permanent alimony. Dawn responded by threatening suicide. To her dismay, instead of getting upset as he usually did at her unhappiness, Jake said "that would certainly change my child support budget."

At that point, Dawn knew it was over. She lost her hold over Jake by not giving him the attention he needed. She never believed Jake would love himself more than he loved her. The attentive lawyer was the conduit for Jake's shift in allegiance. If Dawn had been less self-involved and had deigned to entertain the issues behind Jake's existential questing instead of ignoring them, Jake might still be her husband, maybe still working in the computer industry but at least living a life that both could share and enjoy. Instead, having just passed the bar exam, he's started a new career with a new wife, Lorrie.

Before we move on to taking the pulse of your marriage, consider an exercise based upon a person's philosophy of the future, which Maslow believed could assess where a person was in terms of his needs. Ask your husband what his life (or world, or situation) would be like if money and health were no objects. His answer, according to Maslow, will identify needs that have emerged but that have not been met.

Good Marital Habits

We know from studies performed over the last fifty years that the basis for a close, healthy, satisfying marriage is communication, closeness (emotional and physical), and respect. Marriages marked by these characteristics are generally vital and re-energizing to the individual partners. Spouses in these types of marriages give freely to each other and they gain, in return, a sense of love and security that provides them unique comfort. We know what works, but—perhaps more helpful—we also know what threatens a loving marriage, leaving it vulnerable to outside forces that would tear it asunder.

Unlike some researchers who base their work on self-reported surveys (which if not properly scored can be highly unreliable), John M. Gottman, Ph.D., has spent years in his so-called "love lab" (the Family Research Laboratory in Seattle) watching couples interact and then scoring them based upon their style of communication, interactions, gestures, and physiological signs (heartbeat, perspiration, respiration, blood pressure).

From years of observations, he's derived a theory of the things that make a marriage strong and of what things constitute the marital version of the four horsemen of the apocalypse.

Avoiding Marriage Killers

According to Dr. Gottman, the four marriage killers are *criticism* (attacks on a person's character); *contempt* (perhaps the most corrosive, as it conveys disgust and revulsion); *defensiveness* (preoccupation with blaming or being right over making matters better); and *stonewalling* (the passive-aggressive tendency to distance oneself from the issues at hand such that the person is checked out and no longer present in any meaningful sense). In addition to these four horsemen, however, Gottman found physiological manifestations of trouble. Stress can cause an adrenaline rush (which Gottman calls "flooding"), setting in motion a fight-or-flight response in which emotions overrule calmer, clearer action and situations escalate from bad to horrid.

If criticism, contempt, defensiveness, stonewalling, and flooding are marital poisons, what are helpful behaviors? Gottman suggests the steps in his book, *The Seven Principles for Making Marriage Work*. Marriage boils down to friendship, respect, tenderness, and communion (the act of connecting with your partner's head, heart, and body). Here are the actions Gottman recommends:

1. Mind your spouse's emotional landscape by making a point to know, consider, and respect the things that make him tick. Gottman calls this "maintaining a love map."
2. Keep in mind the reason you fell for your partner in the first place, preserving that positive global view. Gottman calls this "fostering fondness and admiration."
3. Be grateful you have each other, and let your partner know you appreciate him. After all, everyone likes to be appreciated.

When given an opportunity to opt for distance or intimacy, choose the latter every time. Gottman calls this "turning towards, instead of away."

4. Keep an open mind to what your spouse thinks, feels, and believes. You are not always right, and you do not always know best. Gottman calls this "accepting influence." Interestingly, Gottman's research shows that it's more important for a husband to be open to his wife's influence, rather than vice versa, to promote marital happiness.

5. Resolve all the differences you can by using respectful, open, diplomatic methods of communication. (Remember, your body speaks as loudly as your words.) Gottman calls this "solving the solvable."

6. Remember Reinhold Niebuhr's serenity prayer ("God, grant me the serenity to accept the things I cannot change, courage to change the things I can, and the wisdom to know the difference"). Once you've realized what cannot be changed or resolved, find the humor and grace to live with what remains and all it will entail. Gottman calls this tenet "coping with the conflicts you can't resolve."

7. Help each other reach your potential and, as a couple, build a positive, worthy life together. Gottman calls this "creating shared meaning."

Attentive Interaction

Now you know the kinds of emotions and communications that are good for a marriage, as well as those that are not. So how does one communicate in a positive, disarming way? In a nutshell, you listen. Really tune in to what your partner is saying, repeat what you think he said, and if you don't have it right, ask him to keep trying until you get it.

Here, on the facing page, are some communication tips that work well:

- Mind your timing. Don't bring up difficult matters when you can see your spouse is distracted or on overload from unrelated matters. Ask for time when he's ready and able to deal with you and your important matter.
- Keep it simple and stay on point.
- Stay in the moment and on the message.
- When in doubt, try a little tenderness and stay positive.
- No one likes to be maligned or assailed. Discuss issues, not character flaws, unless you're willing to list yours, too, for dissection.
- Be as respectful to your partner as you would with your best friend. (Hopefully, he is your best friend.)

Attentive communication can make all the difference. Consider the case of Diane and Jeff. They decided to see me before they went to the divorce lawyers. It was obvious at the first session that this couple did not speak the same language. The nonverbal communication was louder than their words as they sat opposed to one another, not looking at each other or showing any signs of togetherness. I learned that Diane's mother was a nag who barked orders to her husband and children, and that's what her daughter had learned to do as well. Also, Jeff had been taught to be seen and not heard, so he had no idea how to express his feelings and thoughts. I began treatment with basic communication skills and techniques. Diane and Jeff were eager to learn the tools to hear and be heard without hurting each other. At one point in treatment, Jeff told Diane that he was an adult and could say what he felt and would take responsibility for his words. Diane was thrilled since Jeff's hostile silence and withdrawal in the past always bothered her. Knowing that Jeff would listen, Diane felt she could now ask for what she needed rather than demand it (the way her mother did). The minute Diane opened her mouth, Jeff's anger subsided.

They continued to refine their skills by setting aside a half hour each day to talk and listen to each other. I suggested they use a kitchen timer, allowing each to speak uninterrupted for fifteen minutes. At the end of the half hour they might discuss issues, depending on how they felt. If one needed to address an additional issue, the clock would be set for five more minutes, allowing the other partner the same. They could try to reach a resolution that evening or agree to shelve it for another day, secure that they could discuss openly it later. It was not very long before the experience of speaking and listening began to be a normal part of their communication repertoire. They still have issues, but now they have a process that helps them communicate effectively and respectfully.

So you see, effective communication and sound conflict-resolution skills can be taught. More good news comes from studies that show a link between physical attraction and "communication satisfaction." The better you can listen to your mate and express your feelings, too, the better looking you'll be to him. (You'll find more on effective communication in Chapter 9.) What's more, once you do acquire constructive communication and dispute-resolution skills, the world, not to mention your marriage, will be your oyster.

Shirley Glass, Ph.D., wrote that even happy marriages were vulnerable to outside threats. The data from my years of clinical practice working with couples have yielded a different result. I find that happy (vital, bonded, and satisfied) spouses do not cheat or detach from their marriage unless one of them has a clear propensity for risk taking or, due to a personality disorder, engages in personally destructive or irresponsible behavior (for instance, the classic "sex addict" who tells you that he just can't help himself—read Chapter 6 for more).

In any case, taking action to keep your relationship interesting, engaging, and vital works wonders to inoculate a marriage from potentially noxious outside forces. By reviewing your caregiving techniques, your sexual availability and interests, your willingness to encourage growth, and your communication skills, you have the power to protect what is rightfully yours: your marriage.

How Do You Rate?

If you are interested in measuring your marriage from a social science point of view, visit the PREPARE-ENRICH Program/testing Web site, online at *www.prepare-enrich.com*. There you will find a quick, free test that will give you an idea of how you and your spouse rate on various scales of compatibility, including how you communicate and resolve conflict; how you assess marital roles, responsibilities, and expectations; how you allocate time for individual and joint interests; what attitudes you take toward finances, family, sexuality, parenting, and religion; and how you react to typical life stressors (unexpected setbacks, illness, or loses).

For a fee, the site will also administer the long version of the ENRICH test, and you will receive a lengthy, computer-generated summary of your relationship broken down according to how compatible you are on the various topics. You will learn how, according to your scored results, you and your spouse can work on your identified strengths and overcome the test-detected weaknesses. For those of you who would rather not sit through a battery of tests, the elements of marital satisfaction covered in this chapter are enough to lead you to discuss and resolve issues that, left untended, could fertilize the seeds of future marital discontent.

CHAPTER 2

Telltales of Trouble Brewing

The focus so far has been on the positive aspects of love and how to maintain the love you have. In a perfect world, this book could end now, but in reality dangers lurk without and within. Reading this book might give you wonderful knowledge, insight, and mate-guarding techniques, but it's possible that some damage has already been done in the past, when your actions and/or words were less inviting and more hostile. In this chapter we will review the circumstances that could mean your man has one foot out the door, or at least, reveal a crack in the marital body armor.

Before we look at the telltales of potential trouble, recall what you've read so far. A man's attitude toward his wife and his marriage is premised upon how satisfied he feels in his own skin, day in and day out. If all of his important physical and emotional needs are met, or at least considered, his commitment to his partner increases, and his need to look for attractive alternatives diminishes. A man will devote his time, attention, and money to his wife if she makes him feel good about himself.

The married man will place no value on the "alternatives" out there when he is committed to his relationship (a function of his happiness and contentment). His actions will show that he cares about his wife and will reinforce their bond. Generally, a husband's commitment finds form in continuing, respectful, and honest communication; compromises made to maintain the relationship; and constructive responses to a partner's negative conduct. The last item nips any vitriol in the bud, often gently placing the critical partner on the more favorable path of fairness and civility. In fact, facing a spouse's negative behavior with a positive attitude is one of the ways to implement Gottman's principles (forever focusing on the positive, leaving the insoluble alone, as described in Chapter 1). It is a good way to avoid the four horsemen of the marital apocalypse—criticism, contempt, defensiveness, and withdrawal—and the fight-or-flight response to emotional stress that foreshadow marital distress and, often, divorce.

Finally, the happily committed partner will share tasks and chores that further the goal of marital stability and partner satisfaction, creating a positive feedback loop that protects the marriage from interlopers. For instance, a man will take on

Beauty Opens Doors, but Warmth Keeps the Home Fires Burning

You could be the most beguiling beauty of all time, but if you belittle your mate, he will find someone else who is lovely enough to attract him but who also has the emotional components to make him feel like a prince. Consequently, even the most gorgeous women have to meet their mates' needs, or eventually those men will find an attractive alternative who will unlock the door to their happiness.

more paid work, maintain the yard or the house, do the laundry, or mind the kids to help his mate instead of pursuing an interest that would benefit or please him individually.

So what happens when the worldview is less rosy? According to the experts, when contentment ebbs, and there's a change in attitude toward the relationship or the other mate, the partner who feels more threatened by the breakdown (and possible breakup) is likely to suspect that something's been going on. While that partner might not be correct, there seems to be a built-in bias to sniff out trouble, even if, in fact, there is none. (One expert uses a smoke-detector analogy and says it's better to be more sensitive and save your life, than less sensitive and die from fire.) As a mate, it pays to be overly vigilant and react, than underprotective and lose a spouse. A corresponding thought is expressed in an old Arabic proverb: Trust in Allah, but tie your camel. (You'll read more about camel-tying in later chapters on mate-guarding strategies and behaviors.)

Preludes to Infidelity

Before we dive into the most common infidelity scenarios—or at least the circumstances that should make a mate sit up and take notice of what's going on in front of her, or behind her back—let's discuss the typical life-cycle changes and personal situations that can make a man prone to succumb to temptation. While some lifestyle changes are so well known they've become cliché (think red Corvette, hair dye, newer, hipper clothes, and a gym membership), other, subtler life changes can be equally challenging to a marriage.

First we'll take a look at the most common, the proverbial male midlife crisis (MLC). Typically occurring between the ages of forty and sixty (as your mate's youth wanes and his mortality waxes), it can last anywhere from several months to several years. Commonly, the MLC can make a man suddenly desire things (and people) he's never considered before, such as quitting his job and wife, while gaining a new girl, a new life, and new interests. While not every husband will scrap his life and spouse during these midlife years, many do undergo major physical, psychological, and emotional changes induced by both brain and body chemistry, as well as the inevitable passage of time. Interestingly, some experts believe that from age forty to fifty-five, men's brains become more similar to (or, perhaps, less different than) women's. This could be due to falling sex hormone levels, primarily testosterone (the promoter of risk-taking, aggression, and less sensitivity to pain—emotional and physical). If so, it may mean that midlife could be the beginning of the best time for couples, if they just hang in there and help each other through this challenging life-cycle phase using the information provided here.

How He Was Back When

Frankly, the first crucial test for fidelity is the prenuptial or engagement phase. Depending on his maturity and commitment, a man can feel trapped into doing something at this stage that is expected, but not desired. This problem typically occurs when the fiancé is a young adult, under twenty-five, unprepared emotionally and physically to end his carefree, irresponsible, self-focused lifestyle. In most instances, these men are given an ultimatum by their girlfriends, who are ready to commit and settle down with one man.

Instead of accepting the consequences of rejecting the threat, the young men cave although they resent being boxed in. After the engagement, their resentment continues. In some cases, they act on it in ways that make it impossible for their fiancées to go through with the wedding (think of bachelor parties with women who do more than strip and strut for the groom-to-be).

In cases where the would-be brides persevere, the marriage is in jeopardy of ending from the time it begins. According to Helen Fisher, author of *Anatomy of Love: A Natural History of Monogamy, Adultery, and Divorce,* unless they have children immediately, many of these couples dissolve their unions within five years. Other research has resulted in similar findings. Sometimes the men are able to accept responsibility, lose their resentment, and grow into the role of husbands, while their wives put the past behind them to begin again. If this situation sounds familiar, the future of your relationship depends upon your willingness to forgive and move on, as well as upon your mate's desire to remain married.

A Pregnant Pause in Marriage

Another time when husbands tend to wander, and one that might sound counterintuitive, is when the wife is pregnant. The reasons for cheating are often the same: the husband is not ready for the responsibility of fatherhood, and he wants to reclaim the careless ways of his single days. Due to cultural or social forces, some men have difficulty relating to a pregnant women as a sexual being. Instead of enjoying sex with their pregnant wives, they put her on a pedestal and seek sexual refuge elsewhere. If you suspect this is your man's issue, he needs therapy to explore why he cannot relate sexually to the woman

Suspicions According to one study, though women abhor sexual infidelity, they are particularly anxious about their man's potential emotional bond ("emotional infidelity") with a rival. These women know that once a man connects with another paramour, he is likely to leave for the new lover.

he loves and who is in the bloom of health and fertility carrying his child.

Though the focus of this book is preventing infidelity, it does happen. Later chapters of this book explore how to recover, and what to do after an affair. For now, bear in mind that pregnancy flings are usually more about taking a last stand against domesticity and fleeing from reality than they are about the wife. In any case, learning that your mate had an affair while you were carrying his child can be so traumatic that the broken trust kills the love that once was, irreparably breaking the marriage.

Healing, if it occurs, requires work by both partners. Ultimately, it depends on the wife's power to forgive and move on without harboring the hurt and bitterness that her husband brought upon her. If it's any consolation, the man who has an affair while his mate is pregnant is likely to remain in the marriage. The biological and financial investments are too great, and the social costs of leaving a pregnant wife are enormous.

His Ego Needs

Other times for potential trouble take place when a man experiences professional disappointments—or successes. In the first case, he might be nursing a wounded ego; in the latter, his added prestige brings power, which attracts potential mates ("mate-poachers," to use one researcher's term). Depending upon the status of your relationship, these women might begin to look like "attractive alternatives." Like many men, your husband will most likely make a mental comparison, with what he wants, needs, and gets at home in one column, and what's available to him elsewhere in the other column. Though it's neither nice nor comforting to think about, as the wife, you should make it your business to keep track of your mate's commitment arithmetic. The benefits of your wifely attention are substantial, while the costs of your marital laxity could be devastating. It's your choice.

Your Accomplishments

Another common time for infidelity is when the wife becomes unusually successful and the husband fails to keep pace with her steady rise and accomplishments. These men break their vows for several reasons. First, depending upon the type of relationship they share and the individual personalities involved, a man's masculinity can be threatened as his wife attains more acclaim than he does. If so, the man might find someone else (generally of lesser status than his wife) who will make him feel manly, worthy, and important. If the wife is traveling more or becoming less of a companion to her husband due to new demands at work, or if she has a loss of respect for him at home, the husband might reach out for friendship—and more—from another woman in his circle (think secretary, receptionist, neighbor, workout partner). This is an attempt to restore his self-esteem, diminished by his relative failure in the face of his wife's successes.

The Grinding of Time

The last set of common life-cycle events that can trigger infidelity includes the empty nest syndrome (when all the kids have left the home), the serious illness of a spouse, or the death of parents, siblings, contemporaries, or children. These losses inflict both physical stress and emotional pain. The brevity of life felt at these times can spur a man to take unusual measures to change what remains of his own way of life—and not always for the better. (Sometimes change is just change, not improvement.) For some men in these circumstances, any freedom from feeling mortally vulnerable can bring temporary relief, even if it jeopardizes their marriage. On the other hand, tragic or fateful events can have the opposite effect, keeping couples together. Recall the news stories about people dismissing their divorce cases and reuniting after September 11.

Now let's turn our attention to some scenarios that might make you wonder whether your husband has found a lover, or at least a good friend, outside the marriage.

Tidings of Potential Trouble

Perhaps you have noticed that your spouse's actions and attitudes seem different. Upon reflection, you wonder what he's doing, thinking, and feeling, and with whom. It might be that you're spending less quality time together or are talking less. You both work long hours. The kids require your energy and attention and leave you with little at day's end. Lately, you feel more like housemates than lovers. Maybe the two of you are exhausted and simply experiencing one of the inevitable ebbs of married life. The examples (an aggregate from those I've encountered through my patients) set forth in this section don't necessarily mean your marital bond is broken. Rather, they encompass the classic signs of marital distress, which you ignore at your peril.

Initially, a wife will notice subtle but detectable emotional changes in her mate's emotional tone when he interacts with her. For instance, a husband might not care what his wife says or does. While he doesn't walk away while she's talking, he doesn't engage, he doesn't fight back, and he doesn't complain. He no longer seems interested in his spouse's thoughts or feelings. Though the husband is still coming home each night, and even having sex with her, something is missing: his interest. He's emotionally checked out, even though he's still living with his wife.

After a time of emotional distancing, if things don't return to normal from the wife's point of view, she'll notice next that her husband's actions begin to mirror his distancing emotions. He becomes physically remote, avoiding her or making excuses to be left alone. He forgets significant relationship or personal events like birthdays or anniversaries or social commitments. The husband reduces or eliminates participation in family activities. For instance, he'll stop attending religious services at the house of worship he attended with his wife for years. He'll beg off on kids' school and athletic functions. The wife will detect a pattern in which the mate is now physically separating himself from the home, her, and the children, and committing his time and attention to other matters.

Usually, though not always, the last marital activity affected by a slow withdrawal is sex. Some wives report a marked increase in sexual activity with their spouse just before being abandoned.

On the other hand, much more commonly, the wife will see the husband retreat from her sexually, completing the marital disengagement. The loss of, or decrease in, a spouse's sex drive can be a sign of an affair, or not. A husband's undiagnosed illness, depression, or anger toward his wife can also diminish a couple's physical relationship. In either case, a noticeable change in the quality or quantity of your sex life (involving new techniques, positions, toys, or condoms—perhaps to prevent pregnancy or transmission of his recently acquired sexually

Get Checked   If you've been engaging in sexual contact while or after you've discovered your husband has been with a lover, get yourself tested for AIDS, hepatitis B and C, the human papilloma virus, syphilis, gonorrhea, chlamydia, and any other ailments that your doctor suggests, ASAP.

transmitted infection or disease) requires serious attention and a discussion.

Altered Personal Routines

Another pattern of behavior that can give one pause is changing work hours and responsibilities. As the wife, you know your husband best and should be able to decode his actions. (Is he working more to earn more, or to make time for someone else?) For example, you know how far your spouse drives to work and what kind of miles he puts on the car a week. Suddenly, his odometer reflects greater driving distances—to places and persons unknown. Or he's away on business trips much more frequently than before or is working longer hours—in the evenings, during weekends, and on holidays—without an obvious reason (such as a project that you know about and with which you are comfortable). In these circumstances, a good-natured but concerned conversation with your spouse is in order.

Alibis for Sale While I don't want you to be overly cynical, I've learned from patients that there are Web sites that provide incredibly meticulous alibis for those who need to "get away" for a few days. These services arrange lodging, dining, and transportation through a dummy company so the "client's" (cheater's) credit card is never implicated. In fact, some services will arrange a fake seminar, complete with class photo of fellow attendees, to prove that the cheater really was at a marketing seminar in North Dakota (when he was truly on a beach in St. Bart's with his lover). Think I'm kidding? Get online and check this out: *www.alibinetwork.com.*

New routines that can ring a wife's alarm bells include finding your spouse clearing the computer's cache (eliminating the history of Web pages he's viewed or surfed) after he's used the machine; learning that he's visiting singles-, porn-, or sex-related chat rooms; or discovering that he has set up a private e-mail account on the family computer, which he refuses to let you access even when you ask nicely. Or maybe he's purchased a new laptop so he can surf the Web as he likes, instead of using the family computer.

More cause for concern arises if your husband buys a new cell phone and doesn't give you the number or doesn't use it or answer it in your presence. Or your husband receives phone calls at home and then tells you that he must go out for a drive and returns seven or eight hours later, yet the odometer has hardly changed. Perhaps he hangs up when you enter the room, or you're hung up on when you answer your own phone. Finding receipts for jewelry that you never received, or credit card charges for airlines on which you've not flown, or for hotels you've not stayed in, or finding numbers you don't recognize on phone bills are all reasons to ask him what is happening.

A signal that something might be afoot is a new interest in his physical appearance, especially if your husband never cared less before. In fact, a change in a mate's style of hair or dress—say from conventional, to a newer, hipper look—should certainly raise a wife's eyebrow. Similarly, drastic and sudden weight loss and exercise regimes may signal a spouse is ready for a change, in his body and, maybe, in his lover's. Unless this new-found narcissism follows a regimen you know about or a health threat that requires a change in diet and exercise, something could be going on and the change deserves your inquiry.

When you share your concerns about these behaviors, your husband might grow angry or defensive, or he might tell you that nothing's wrong and it's all in your head, while the behaviors continue without satisfactory explanation. In that case, you have every right to press the issue. You are his wife and you have the right—and he has the obligation—to tell you what he's doing, why, where, when, and with whom. Remember, good marriages require open, honest communication, and trust. Not blind trust—that's faith, and at this point he doesn't deserve it. You, of course, will reciprocate if asked for similar information.

Separate Pursuits

If the routines aren't enough to make you stop and think, when a husband decides that he can only have fun or enrichment without you, it's a sure sign that he's making a statement and staking an individual path. Consider the following examples:

Getting individual counseling: Many a patient has sought counseling or therapy before leaving home as a way of gaining approval from an authority figure (in this case, the counselor) to prove that he was doing the right thing.

Improving the inner self: An unanticipated interest in mind-expanding activities (like attending museum exhibitions, or readings, or signing up for acting, art, or film classes) that exclude you could be a sign that your husband is just broadening his horizons—or it could signal that he's preparing for a new life, and possibly a new love.

New sports: Your husband takes up hobbies or physical activities (skiing, sailing, biking, fishing) that require his absence or place him in the company of people who don't know you—and aren't necessarily friends of your marriage—and you are not invited to join the fun.

Even if you notice *all* of these signs in your husband, it doesn't necessarily mean your marriage is doomed and headed for divorce (particularly if these signs aren't accompanied by drastic changes in family finances, addressed next). Rather, it may mean you need to make the time to talk about where he's headed and how he sees you fitting into the picture, so that as a couple you can benefit from his experiences. Maintain interest in your husband and be part of his life.

Financial Changes

There are behaviors that let you know your marriage, or your mate, needs attention. Then there are behaviors that more or less say that it's over. Though the more dangerous warning signs are obvious in hindsight, they're often overlooked at the time they occur—particularly if you're not suspecting a problem. These well-planned activities typically affect a couple's financial assets and can mean real trouble for a wife, whether there's a romantic rival on the scene or not. Collectively, this kind of conduct is referred to as "divorce planning." Here's a list of things to watch for:

- Your mate reroutes mail that used to come to the house, so that you no longer receive his financial information, like his cell phone bill, bank, credit card, or brokerage statements.
- For no apparent reason, your partner decides to open his own account when you used to maintain a joint checking account.
- Your mate reroutes pay from a joint account to an individual account that you don't have access to.
- If your mate owns or operates his own business or professional practice and he suddenly reduces his draw, and you

experience an abrupt decrease in money to the household from that entity.

- Your partner suddenly relies on joint credit cards or home equity lines of credit to pay normal household expenses (the mortgage on the home, rent, or other ordinary budget items) that were regularly paid from current income, or he asks you to start paying expenses that he formerly paid or contributed to.

- Your husband raids his individual retirement accounts or employment-related assets without consulting you.

- Your partner wants to refinance your home mortgage, to withdraw a substantial amount of cash for a purpose that is suited more to your husband's benefit, as opposed to a purpose that is clearly for your—or your family's—collective benefit or mutual goal.

- Your husband catches "RAIDS" (recently acquired income deficiency syndrome), becoming voluntarily unemployed—or "underemployed"—or he elects to take an early retirement without your approval.

- A transfer of marital assets (like a business, stock, or a professional practice) to your family, relations, friends, or business associates. The legal terminology for this conduct is "entity structuring" or the "separation of ownership from assets," which serves to insulate your mate from personal liability against future creditors (that would be you).

A Cry for Help

Instead of signaling the end of your marriage or relationship, your mate may be experiencing the classic midlife—or other life cycle—crisis and is crying out for help, or, at the least, for couples counseling. In a perfect world, your husband would be able to tell you of his feelings and thoughts, and you would hear him and respond with loving care, but this is not always what happens. Many times, intervention by a mutually selected psychological professional or a trusted, trained clergyperson— or even a good friend with insight and your best interests at heart—can be the key to restoring the vitality of a marriage. These third parties can help figure out what went wrong and how you can get back on track to a loving, loyal, mutually supportive, affectionate, affirmative, complementary, communicative relationship—or not. Read on.

Part 2

MARITAL HAZARDS AND HUSBAND TRAPS

CHAPTER 3

The Ready Replacement Pool

Here, the discussion switches from examining the subject of your vigilance (your man) to delineating the reason for your mate-guarding strategies. I'll be calling her by various tags: the other woman, mate-poacher, marital intruder, trespasser, or interloper. But no matter what she's called, you'll know exactly who she is from her actions and intentions: a homewrecker by any other name.

Why She Wants Your Man

Before we delve into the physical and psychological worlds of the would-be husband snatcher, it would help to nod back to the evolutionary reason why we humans do some of the things we do. Unfortunately, poaching another's partner is a common human practice, though the way it's done varies according to the gender of the poacher. Men are more overtly aggressive, while women are infinitely more subtle and devious when they set out to steal another's mate. In fact, the well-known mate-stealing tactic known as "wedging" (when the interloper strives to get in between you and your man) is often attempted by a so-called friend.

Bear in mind that the impulse to steal your man (especially if he's worth having), is as old as humanity—and your impulse to fight to keep him is just as timeless. I think Dr. Helen Fisher (the media savvy, evolutionary anthropologist) explained the situation best as she answered a question about the rivalry women have towards each other. Here's the exchange from a Salon.com interview for an article titled "The End of Girltalk?":

Tracy Quan (reporter): "Are we in denial about the animosity that exists between females?"

Dr. Fisher: "Yes. Primatologists have discovered what American women somehow have missed: Women are in direct competition with other women. This whole thing of getting together for women's rights has clouded our eyes to the Darwinian nature of 'survival of the fittest.' Women will compete with other women just as men will compete with other men, and they do it very cleverly."

And if that's dialogue is not enough to make you squirm, here's more grist for the feminist mill. The lesbian immersion journalist Norah Vincent disguised herself as a man for a year and a half to experience twenty-first-century American life from an authentically male point of view. In her book, *Self-Made Man: One Woman's Journey into Manhood and Back*, Vincent describes the nature of male camaraderie and how women come off to men as "dates." One of her findings: Men don't kick you when you're down. They want to win, but only when you're feeling at your best. Women, on the other hand, are more devious, wanting to win at any costs—so consider yourself warned. (In the following chapters, you'll also be armed, locked and loaded, prepared to shoot your fellow hunter.) Vincent also found that contrary to the notion that women want a sensitive male—that old cliché of the quiche-eating guy—what they really crave is a "manly" man.

Need more information to get your attention? In the mid 1980s, sociologist Laurel Richardson wrote about the new other woman being a single woman between the ages of twenty-five and forty. Richardson theorized that the phenomenon of the single woman/married man affair had several roots. First, these were the baby boom women who'd come of age just as the women's movement was taking off, thus providing these females with unprecedented opportunities to control their educational, professional, and reproductive lives, unlike any generation of women before them. Second, there was a dearth of similarly educated, ambitious, worthy guys out there. Third, for many, such secret arrangements served their temporary needs.

In all, back then, Richardson found that 18 to 32 percent of single women would become romantically attached to another woman's husband. Richardson predicted that this trend would not only continue but mushroom due to simple demographics: the more single women in the workplace, the less eligible men

The Cassandra of Her Time

Though Richardson wrote her book, *The New Other Woman: Contemporary Single Women in Affairs with Married Men*, more than two decades ago, in it she warned of the coming trend: that an affair between a single woman and a married man would become a social fact, as ubiquitous in the culture as getting married. She was prescient. In 2000, Richard Tuch, MD, wrote about the single woman/married man phenomena as a "syndrome," complete with its own etiology, symptoms, and outcomes.

there are. These girls would take the men they found, even if they happened to belong to someone else.

Neighbors and Sisters and Friends—Oh My!

Now you have a general understanding of the types of women who want your man and why; now let's consider who they are in your life and where they might live. According to Dr. Helen Fisher, "You've got to pick your friends [wisely], and it's remarkable how many women don't! It's stunning." Truer words were never spoken.

Just as most automobile accidents occur within a five-mile radius of home, many marriages are broken by interlopers within the couple's inner circle of acquaintances: someone from the workplace, a neighbor, or a girlfriend of the eventually betrayed spouse. In this situation, we're talking about *your* pal or—with a nod to Carly Simon—the wife of (your husband's) close friend.

Why does betrayal occur so often between friends? Because we tend to befriend people who are much like us. We are attracted to those who are similar to us in values, intelligence, education, interests, and even physical appearance. The professionals call this selection process "positive assortment." Unfortunately, picking friends who are like us means we bring attractive alternates (who share many of our own special attributes) right into the hearth of our lives, closest to our families, and of course, our partners. Not only are our friends desirable (after all, we picked them in our own image), they are close, they are familiar, and they can be the worst possible enemy of your marriage (think Trojan Horse, wolf in sheep's clothing, fox guarding the chicken coop—you get the idea).

Think about it: Your friends have ample access, open opportunity, and, in some cases, no boundaries. Let's examine access first.

Beware Your New Best Friend

Who more than a trusted friend enjoys the benefit of unfettered physical access around your house, your husband, your kids? No one. Your good pal also has emotional entrée and is probably welcome at your home whenever she has a problem, needs a hand, or wants to play a set of tennis. If you are busy, no problem. Your husband is willing to help, for your sake, of course (and initially, it's true). Unfortunately, researchers tell us, and experience proves, that men like variety and that women employ poaching as a mate-getting strategy. (In one study, more than half the women questioned admitted they'd tried to poach another woman's mate for themselves.)

Research also shows us that familiarity fosters positive feelings. The so-called "propinquity effect," from the Latin *propinquitas,* meaning "nearness," gives name to the reality that familiarity and repeated exposure to a person breeds liking—at least initially. In other words, the closer proximity your mate has to a stimulus—your neighbor, your pal, your sister—the more favorably he will view her. Interestingly, this only seems to happen when the beholder's initial feelings about the "stimulus" are neutral. Think about the very interesting and dangerous implications of the propinquity effect as it concerns those near to you—and your husband. Last year, your husband was being honest when he told you that your best friend didn't strike him one way or the other. Yet, after her divorce was final, he began to form an attraction to her. Her proximity over time made her more attractive in his eyes.

Access Equals Opportunity

Next, let's explore what friends, neighbors, and even sisters share with you: plenty of physical and emotional opportunities to share time and space with your mate. Now that you know nearness can make the heart grow founder, your job as the wife is to see that your friends don't take advantage of the intimate knowledge they have about your weaknesses and insecurities and your relationship's vulnerabilities. You can do this by limiting their opportunity to pounce when they know your mate is susceptible to seduction.

You are the wife, and one of your proper prerogatives is to control those who enjoy familiar, informal status in your household due to their address, their blood, or their relationship with you—or your husband. For instance, if you think your sister seems to want too much of your man's attention, just say no. Or if you think your neighbor is showing too much interest in your husband or is advertising her new plastic surgery in a way that makes it pretty clear she's available, put an end to her access. Don't allow or encourage a girlfriend to flirt, flaunt her attractiveness, or offer sexual innuendo toward your husband. Those behaviors are disrespectful to you and your marriage, and they may be an outright, in-your-face come-on to your mate.

You can and must act to prevent your rival from taking further steps to seduce your spouse. Keep her at a distance and share your observations with your husband, denigrating her for her efforts—dissing a rival is a well-known mate-protection strategy—so he can keep his distance, too. Get upset, make a fuss, and be sensitive to deception. Recent studies have shown that when it comes to protecting your mate from the designs of a same sex friend, neighbor, relative, or colleague (your "intrasexual rivals"), you are best to—as Dr. Fisher warns—select better company. Barring that, react quickly to behavior that makes you uncomfortable, gives you pause, or is a blatant mate-stealing maneuver. In the meantime, be very aware that all is fair in love as in war, and deception runs rampant in both.

How do you select better associates? For starters, keep your "single and looking" friends at a safe distance from your partner.

The same holds true for married buddies who are known for sexual promiscuity or adulterous behavior. You want a circle of genuine friends who are desirable and trustworthy. The attractive divorcee down the hall who needs someone to help her install her computer—forget about it. Tell her your husband is permanently out of town and off limits.

Trust your gut, and ban behavior when you feel or believe that a woman is giving your mate cues, whether obvious or subtle, that she's interested in him and potentially available. One way to act on your concern is to let the offender know that you sense (or have seen) what she's up to and that you are fully prepared to take action to protect your marriage and make her pay (in whatever way would be costly to her) if she persists. At this stage, the friendship is probably over. If this person is your sister, well, I'd suggest taking a time out, perhaps for a few years. In any event, realize that if a woman in your personal sphere walks like a mate-stealer, talks like a mate-stealer, and dresses and acts like a mate-stealer, guess what: She's probably a mate-stealer, notwithstanding her verbal assurances to the contrary. Do what's best for you and your marriage. Take her aside and tell her what you see. If she does not back off, ditch her.

As for your husband's female friends, unless they are completely uninterested, it's a good idea for you to go along during any social encounters. Some experts go so far as to suggest eliminating those woman friends. While that may or may not be sensible, you should keep your ears and eyes open. If a female friend is mentioned a tad too much, and then suddenly not at all, that can be a sign of trouble. Make it your business to stake your wifely ground by going to his work and meeting your husband for lunch or, better yet, after work for drinks or dinner. Let this women see he is yours and you are his and that your relationship is strong, healthy, and worth fighting for. If necessary, have a nice chat with her so she knows where you both stand: You are in the inside, she is on the outs. (More on this strategy in Chapter 9.) Your husband can second you, if she has any doubt.

By the way, don't be fooled or lulled into complacency because your girlfriend or your neighbor or your sister (or husband's female friend) is not as beautiful as you are. Not every potential hazard to your happy home is the obvious, over-the-top, Pamela Anderson-esque bombshell. In my practice, I've seen many men ensnared by available, unattractive women after their pretty wives made the devastating mistake of assuring themselves that their husbands would never be attracted to someone so seemingly ordinary. Wrong. The average-looking woman overcomes her physical imperfections by honing her interpersonal skills—including her sexual prowess. She becomes an enchantress because of how she makes her man feel when he's with her.

Think about it. The plain woman has never been beautiful, so she's had a lifetime to cultivate her capacity for warmth, empathy, nurturing, and sexual pleasuring. These are precisely the traits a man can yearn for in a second (or subsequent) companion if his wife was great mating material but now seems incapable of the emotional depth or sexual experience he craves.

For this kind of man, the unattractive woman's psychological features and adventurous physicality can far outweigh the fact that the world at large sees her face as plain or unattractive. Luckily for you, in order for the "plain Jane" to make her move, she must get close enough to your husband to connect with him and arouse his interest. This is where the wifely high boundaries come into play. As the spouse, you are the rightful gatekeeper to your husband and your home. You're job is to see to it that your plainer friend, neighbor, or sister never gains the type of face time with your husband that will allow her to spin a web of empathy and raw sexual availability. If you are not giving him what he needs, what he's tried to tell you he desires, or what you have ignored in his requests, he could be vulnerable to just about anyone's bid to play for free—at least that's the way it begins.

Finally, we know that people tend to marry mates who are relatively equivalent in attractiveness, intelligence, education, values, and goals. Your homely neighbor might know that your husband is out of her league for a long-term commitment. But she might also know that sexually, she has something to offer in the short term, if she can just get close enough to make him feel the affair would be low risk (that is, he won't get caught) and worthwhile. Many a woman snags a man with that very premise, only to push for the longer-term commitment that she really wants once she's bedded him. This maneuver is the evolutionary equivalent to the old bait-and-switch trick that, according to research, has been an effective mate-poaching strategy ever since there have been mates to poach. If you—the wife—catch on and divorce him, he becomes available for her.

Once again, prevention is the key and the cure. Keep your marital boundaries solid and your tolerance for betrayal at zero by female friends from your private ranks if they show any signs of interest in your husband. Let them go out and prey on another man, in another marriage with a less vigilant wife.

Old Flames and Opportunists

Having addressed some of the most common sources of martial trespassers, we come upon the next source of potential trouble: the old girlfriend who's suddenly single and available. Simply because she's no longer married and wants to renew an old friendship, a woman like this might seek contact with your husband after a high school reunion or search for him out of the blue over the Internet or by private investigator. The fact that the focus of her hunt might be married to you doesn't really matter much to her if she's in predatory mode.

Your husband should be telling you about this contact. If he does not and innocently responds, her next move is often an invitation to meet for lunch or drinks—and you will not be on the guest list.

At this point, if your husband goes further and accepts without telling you, he's already crossed the line and allowed an interloper to place a foot in what should be private marital territory. By keeping such contact a secret, he's engaged in serious deception and broken one of the primary conventions required for a good marriage: open and truthful communications. If you find out about this sort of covert activity, you have to tell him that he's making you feel like the outsider in your own marriage and you would like him to include you in all the news from his old pals.

A Sample Note to Stay Away

Dear Madam X:

My husband and I have asked you nicely to stop contacting him at work, at home, and during his day via the cell phone number you paid an investigator to obtain for you illegally. You have decided to ignore our requests and persist on your course of unwanted conduct and interference in our lives. If you do not stop your intrusive actions at once, we will take the appropriate legal steps to protect ourselves from your continued harassments. In addition to filing a criminal complaint, we will seek civil remedies at law and in equity for your intentional violation of our privacy. Please be guided accordingly.

Mrs. I Have Him You Can't

If he responds by apologizing and telling you everything about her contact, including follow-ups and meetings, and invites you along, then she might legitimately be a friend of you mate and your marriage. If he reacts defensively or fails to disclose the facts of the contact, get your mate-guarding engine in gear. You may even consider writing a letter to state your feelings.

If it's clear that you are excluded from her agenda and the old flame is after your man, you have to be prepared to act to make your position as alpha woman perfectly clear. Though the old gal pal might have the advantage of history with your man, don't let their past intimidate your future together as a couple. She's banking on being able to trigger your husband's idealization of his youth in order to devalue his current life (meaning you and your relationship).

If your mate was at his happiest in high school or college, an old flame from that era can try to capitalize on that wistful brand of nostalgia and the memories that, over time, can become what they never were in the past. Or, if they really were the high school couple of the year, king and queen of the prom—or what have you—she will be ready with their old photos or songs in an effort to bring him back to that time of their shared youth, innocence, strength, health, and optimism. How do you counter the heavy weight of reminiscence? By bringing him back to the present, by reminding him of *your* history as a married couple, how he proposed to you, how you had your children—or did whatever it is that you two did that was special and meaningful.

The most psychologically effective technique to neutralize an old flame is to highlight the strengths of you and your relationship and negate your nemesis in a way that preserves your husband's view of himself. You want to diminish her in his eyes, not him in his eyes. In this situation you must be careful not to devalue his youth as you devalue the pest from his past. You may want to (believe it or not) throw a compliment toward the old flame. If you've only seen her from old photos, try something subtle like "for her day, she had the right hairdo" hoping she hasn't changed her style since then. If you've seen her recently as well, and want to be coy, you may say, "She was a cute girl, somehow nature was not kind to her. People would never believe you were the same age."

If you've never seen her at all, no problem. Take the same tack and verbally—this is the tactic women excel at, so use it—denigrate her in a way that makes her seem far less than anyone that your man would ever be interested in. For instance, if she persists in her attempts to contact him or meet him while knowing that he's in a committed relationship with you, you might try saying something like, "She doesn't seem to respect boundaries" or "I wonder if she realizes how she comes off when she goes after a married guy." These kinds of statements let your man know that you are not intimidated by this woman from way back when and that you think she lacks grace, couth, and good common sense each time she reaches out for your guy in her apparent desperation.

Now, after addressing the enemy, follow up by complimenting your man. If this has not been your practice, now is the time to start. If your husband is like most humans, he enjoys receiving compliments. The old flame is most likely handing them out right and left. You know him best, so comment on something you know he considers himself good at. Perhaps he fancies himself a great chef or lover. Make your compliments real and personal and therefore better. Don't lie or give him accolades for something he doesn't do well. This will only make you seem desperate, and he will lose trust in you.

In summary, treat your husband's old flame as you would any other female rival who is trying to disrupt your marriage.

Act immediately to shore up the marital borders, and be sensitive to her continued attempts to reignite a fire with your husband. Let down your mate-guarding only when you are assured that she is out of the picture. Don't ever forget: You have the standing, the status, and the right as the wife or rightful partner to set the limits and maintain your union's intimate boundaries. Let the old flame burn out by letting her know that you are on to her, that you are her superior, and that unlike her, you have a happily married husband or bonded mate.

Turn-About Is Unfair Play (Now That You're the Wife)

So what do you do if your husband left his previous wife for you? Or, put another way, what if you were a poacher yourself and are in the ironic position of having to guard against your own marital interloper?

Use your experience to your advantage. As it takes one to catch one, you can be an affair-detective extraordinaire. If you see him doing to you what he did to your predecessor (when he courted you as a married man) you have every reason to be cautious and on guard. When people say that a leopard doesn't change its spots or a zebra doesn't change its stripes, they are describing the psychological issue of character. If Heraclitus is correct and "man's character is his destiny," you might say that your mate's character can predict the destiny of your relationship or marriage.

But don't despair. Just because he cheated on his wife to meet and marry you doesn't mean you'll suffer the same fate. Most people develop as they grow and mature, with the ability to alter their behavior if they choose. While traits may remain constant, people's moral compasses can shift from barely there to reliably conscientious as they gain age and experience. The most effective way to stop infidelity—regardless of the genesis of your union—is to identify the ways in which your relationship is vulnerable and address them using open communication and positive conflict resolution skills.

If your marriage or your husband is filled with tension or afflicted by stressors, one of the ways he can find release is to be with someone who makes him feel relaxed and comfortable. Knowing that he's opted for adultery before, you know to keep the lines of communication open and be sensitive to his stress level and coping ability. Make it clear that you are there for him and expect him to honor the exclusive bond between you. It might help to remind him that he made the most drastic of life changes to be with you (leaving a prior mate, and perhaps, family) and now that you are a pair, you expect him to make your relationship a priority and a success.

The Other Man—OM

Though most humans would classify themselves as heterosexual, many researchers are convinced that humans have varying sexual impulses (or desires) that vary along a continuum from strictly heterosexual to strictly homosexual. The further along the scale to strictly homosexual, the stronger the individual has the impulse to seek a relationship (emotional, physical, intellectual) with someone of the same sex. The same is true of the opposite. Some people find themselves right in the middle of that scale and as a result desire women as much as men. These people would call themselves bisexual. Sometimes, their desire for one sex over another will depend upon their age or stage in life or simply the individual who arouses them, whether male or female. (Angelina Jolie has said this.)

Most situations involving a male-male-female triangle are instigated by the husband—not the lover—who cannot tamp down his urge for sex and communion with a male companion. Amity Pierce Buxton, author of *The Other Side of the Closet: The Coming-Out Crisis for Straight Spouses and Families,* estimates that over 2 million U.S. marriages are between straight and either bisexual or gay spouses.

There are many pop culture/celebrity examples of marriages in which the woman learned that her husband's lover was a man, including former New Jersey Governor James McGreevey, who had an affair with Mr. Golan Cipel. *Rolling Stone* publisher Jann Wenner left his wife in 1994 to take up with a former CK model, Matt Nye. Though those men's marriages ended, many others continue, and even flourish, though with different ground rules than before. Leonard Bernstein left his wife for Tom Cothran but returned to her four years later.

Whether your marriage can be saved, and under what circumstances, depends upon whether your husband sees himself as gay, bi, or primarily hetero but explorative and curious. (Per their own reports, men such as Hugh Heffner, David Bowie, and Mick Jagger dabbled in homosexual experiences in the 1970s.) Research reveals if a man identifies himself as bisexual, he will typically marry a woman, but to satisfy his homoerotic urges, will find men with whom to have casual sex.

Unlike the situation in which your rival is a woman, you will not be able to compete with another man, no matter how well you communicate or resolve your conflicts. Some couples accommodate the situation within their marriage by agreeing to participate in sexual role-playing in an effort to satisfy the homosexual cravings within the marriage; or they accept that the husband will need sex with men in the future; or the man decides to suppress or ignore his homosexual impulses completely. If, on the other hand, your husband is coming out of the closet after reaching a point in his life where he can no longer deny who he is and how he lives—or wants to live—there's not much you can do to stop him, nor should you.

Ultimately, what you do when your man desires men will depend upon what you believe you require, what you want, and how committed you are to each other versus what you cannot abide. You will generally need support, and often therapy. You will find out you are not alone and this event is not about you—though you are deeply involved and probably hurt and feeling betrayed. For superb local resources on how to handle this difficult issue, go online to the Straight Spouse Network (SSN) at *www.straightspouse.com*.

Part-Time Lovers

Now let's consider a different marital hazard: the part-time mistress. Unlike the wife wanna-be, this type of marital trespasser comes in two varieties, the lifer and the flinger.

The Lifer

The lifer is the woman who hangs in there, aware that your spouse will not divorce you. Many politicians have had lifers. Most famously, the late French president François Mitterrand had not only a lifer, but an illegitimate daughter by her. On the Western front, Katherine Hepburn was Spencer Tracy's lifer. Famous aviator Charles Lindbergh had a lifer—or two, or three—each with children. Even the famously nerdy *On the Road* reporter Charles Kuralt had his own lifer tucked away in Montana. No one was the wiser till she filed a legal claim against his estate. (More on legal troubles connected with paramours in Chapter 13.)

Though she might be litigious upon a lover's death, the lifer is generally satisfied with whatever time and energy your husband will offer her while he's breathing. She understands that your husband has other commitments to you and your family and that he'll never, ever leave you for her. If you do divorce, however, it's a different ball game—witness the arc of the love affair between Prince Charles and Camilla Parker Bowles, his lover then lifer-turned-wife.

Why would a woman accept the unfulfilling role of lifer? On the whole, it's a matter of low self-worth. The lifer believes her part-time arrangement with your husband is the best that she can attain with a man of your mate's rank, or she'd demand more for herself. The lifer serves at your mate's convenience, and, derivatively yours and your family's, and she knows it. When your husband's able to meet, they meet. When he's not able, he cancels, even at the last minute. There are no questions; there are no excuses. She understands her place in the triangle. The lifer is always on·call and never on firm ground.

Children are rarely the fruit of this union, as most men don't want illegitimate heirs, so she's rarely a mother, unless she's had kids before. Despite all the drawbacks to this complicated arrangement, the lifer can be around forever unless she has an epiphany—or a shot of self-esteem. Or your husband might seek counseling on his own; or you and your husband might seek joint therapy that results in her being jettisoned from the marital relationship; or you divorce and move on. Oddly, however, many men marry a brand-new girlfriend if their marriages end, leaving their lifers lost, older, bitter, and full of resentment.

The Flinger

On the other end of the part-time poacher spectrum is the flinger. Commonly, this brand of husband snatcher has a busy career or social life (or both). This is the kind of woman highlighted in Laurel Richardson's book *The New Other Woman: Contemporary Single Women in Affairs with Married Men*. Unlike the other woman who wants your husband to leave you so she can step into your wifely shoes, the flinger wants your marriage to continue so her personal life remains undisturbed. She'll have your cake and eat hers too. Flingers require absolute autonomy to enjoy romance, excitement, and secrets with your husband. In fact, the elements of mystery, danger, and adventure are the glue holding this relationship together.

This part-time lover steals time with your man to escape the mundane, but nothing more. She's in it for the good times while maintaining her freedom. The flinger does not desire your daily wifely duties. She will, however, partake of your wifely privileges including having passionate sex with your mate, sharing his most intimate fantasies and desires, dining out with him, traveling surreptitiously together to exotic places, and—depending on her circumstances—enjoying your husband's financial, professional, and (or) emotional support for the time they are an item.

Interestingly, despite its apparent lack of depth, the recreational poacher, a.k.a. flinger, is no less a danger to your marriage than the woman who wants to be your husband's next wife. The friskier and more independent the flinger is, the tamer and more needy you seem by comparison. She's the girlfriend and you're the old lady—no matter who's older than whom. She'll dazzle your husband with her nautical skills aboard a sailboat off the coast of Catalina, while you are home, tired and haggard from staying up all night with your sick child. He'll be besotted by her energy and feel weighed down by your anxiety. It's hard to compete—at first—when the flinger snatcher offers fantasy, while you represent real life with its everyday hassles. There's nothing fair about the flinger's approach, but there are ways to ward her off.

Fortunately, the flinger's sense of timing is as finely hewn as her self-interest. She's apt to leave your man within a year, just as the magic between them begins to wane. By then, she'll have found someone new to provide the adventure and variation she craves from an illicit liaison. Her mantra? If the thrill is gone, it's over. But that doesn't necessarily mean it's over for you. An affair with a part-time snatcher (who dumps your husband before he's ready for the breakup) can leave him wistful and wanting her long after she's split. Your mate's remnant longing for the flinger is never good for a marriage and generally requires therapy to address—and treat—the reasons he made the leap to infidelity in the first place, and why he pines for someone who used him, while hurting a wife to whom he is legally and morally, if not emotionally, committed. (All manner of couples therapy is explored in Chapter 10.)

Finally, know that flingers come in different flavors and from all walks of life. Contrary to conventional wisdom, most flingers are not Angelina Jolie clones. Many are ordinary-looking soccer moms, executives, teachers, nurses, or housewives with an appetite for something new, with someone new. And don't be lulled into thinking that your man's snatcher-safe because he would never go for a flinger type. Remember, a craving for variety and novelty fuels the fling. So, in an ironic way, the more different the flinger is from you—or from his type—the stronger the attraction, at least for a while. We look at ways to protect your marriage from the flinger, as well as other snatchers, in the following chapters.

CHAPTER 4

Knowing Your Rival's Psyche

Now that you know that there are other women (and, perhaps, a few men) who want your guy, examining their psychology will provide insight into who some of them are and why they do what they do. First, let's consider that most people don't want to become involved with a married man—especially if there are children involved—if there are single alternatives available. It's a complicated situation that nearly everyone frowns upon. (Additionally, it's expensive in both emotional and financial terms—most humans would prefer to stick hot needles in their eyes than to carry the stigma of home-wrecker.)

So, given the societal norms that value marriage and family—and frown upon those who would tear it asunder—why would another woman place herself squarely in the middle of trouble? Because in some cases, it's convenient—recall the flinger—and, in the end, she doesn't really want to steal your guy; she just wants to borrow him. In other cases, people meet and believe it's kismet or fate that brought them together, notwithstanding all the pain they might cause a spouse or kids. Then, there are the women born after 1945 who are just dealing with demographics, that there are fewer men around than women.

These kinds of rivals are often easier to ward off than the hardcore mate-poacher, who will go for your guy because taking men, no matter what the cost to him, her, or you, is simply what she does. In many cases, I've found that the woman who deliberately wrecks another's marriage with a devil-may-care attitude has a psychological condition—a personality disorder (known in the psych business as a PD) or other psychological condition, like bipolar disorder—that compels her to ignore or even flout the collective rules and customs that bind the rest of us in society. In other words, this kind of other woman has thought processes (not beauty, brains, or bucks, as you might have imagined) that separate her from you and the rest of the non-neurotic world. In this chapter we'll examine what to expect should a poacher with a personality disorder appear on the scene.

A Wife's Guide to Personality Disorders

Generally, a personality disorder refers to a cluster of fixed traits (ways of thinking, feeling, relating, acting, and reacting) that a person exhibits as he or she meets with varied personal and social circumstances. People with personality disorders think, feel, see, and react to social situations predictably—and unsuitably—in ways that the rest of us would not. These inappropriate thoughts and behaviors interfere with an individual's ability to function as effectively as she might otherwise in the world because she is at odds with the cultural norm.

We live among people with personality disorders every day. Gaining insight into their motivations and psychological operating systems should help you protect yourself or your marriage if or when an interloper with a personality disorder crosses your or your husband's path. The different kinds of personality disorders are fully described in the *Diagnostic and Statistical Manual of Mental Disorders,* Fourth Edition (DSM-IV), published by the American Psychiatric Association. This is the volume that every mental-health professional—psychiatrist, psychologist, and social worker alike—uses to diagnosis and decide on treatment for his or her patients. The DSM-IV is the bible for every therapist.

Many personality disorders overlap each other and share a number of components. Keep this in mind as we look at the narcissistic personality disorder, the borderline personality disorder, and the antisocial personality disorder, the three most common and problematic marital trespassers. Runners-up would be the histrionic personality disorder (the drama queen, similar to the narcissist, whose actions are designed to create high drama and focus all eyes on her, at all times, at all costs) and the dependent personality disorder (clinging vine, more commonly identified as a dependent personality who relies upon others for her existence). The dependent personality disorder is discussed in depth in Chapter 6.

Narcissists—Loving Themselves and Your Husband

A narcissist is someone who is only interested in her needs. The people in her path are there to serve her and maintain her inflated sense of self. She comes before all and has no interest in or ability to consider how others might feel or be affected by her behavior. She simply doesn't give a damn and as a result is a danger zone for all around her, especially those in her close circle. She will manipulate without shame or regret to get what she wants. She is motivated by the need for attention, adoration, devotion, and praise rather than propriety, decency, honor, or regard for her fellow man—and certainly not woman.

A big gold band on the left ring finger of a married man is meaningless to a narcissist on the prowl, except to signal that this guy is probably healthy, safe, and knows how to make a commitment—a good thing as far as she's concerned. While not all mate-poachers are card-carrying narcissists, many are. As you'll learn, the best way to fend off the narcissistic poacher is to stop her before she starts. As in most cases of attempted marital trespass, the best defense is a good offense.

A narcissist will present several challenges to you and your husband. First, there aren't many of them, so most people are unfamiliar with their tactics. Narcissists account for less than 1 percent of the population. Most (between 50 to 75 percent) are male, but when they are female, watch out. To put the DSM-IV info into ordinary language, she will be filled with fantasies of unlimited influence and success. Her self-view doesn't mean that she has the goods to back up her agenda, but it does mean she has an almost unearthly drive and the emotional energy to try to make her dreams come true. That is where the danger lies. Narcissists will try to achieve their goals, no matter how grandiose or exaggerated, and no matter who gets hurt. Highly egotistical, the narcissist believes that she is "special" and should only be in the company of other exceptional people. This kind of mindset gives the new staffer the guts to approach your husband with consummate comfort and ease. She sees him as an equal of sorts since she has an exaggerated sense of her own achievements and talents.

The narcissists of the world expect to be recognized as extraordinary, even superior, notwithstanding their lack of talent, credentials, or experience. A narcissist will take advantage of whomever she can to get her needs met. If that means going for your husband, watch out. How will she implement the takeover plan? She may become best friends with your husband's assistant to gain access to his office. Once she's attained physical proximity, next she'll go for closeness. Once in range, a narcissist will strike directly—forget the subordinate—by doing something seemingly innocent, like giving your man an innocuous, inexpensive gift; perhaps a desk clock or picture frame for your kids' picture. (Who could quarrel with this? After all, they're your kids, too, right? Wrong.)

If your husband accepts her seemingly inoffensive offering, this woman will continue her pursuit, only ratcheted up a notch. Remember, a woman with a narcissistic personality disorder doesn't labor under the conventions that bind most of us. What's more, your husband is clueless at this point, sensing no danger from the interloper's friendly gesture. So when a narcissist engages him in a personal conversation about his wife (you), she's gaining valuable information to help her assess your weak spots. Family and kids are outwardly safe conversational material, so he has no sense that she's moving in for more. That's when she strikes.

Borderlines—Desperately Seeking Your Husband

If you think narcissists are tough, let's examine the other woman with a borderline personality disorder. "Borderline" in this context means she is on the fringe of various diagnoses. She's not psychotic (which we'll discuss last), but she's chaotic and anxious, suffering from impaired functioning from her poor self-image and worldview of others as cold, abandoning, and callous.

First, the borderline other woman is extremely demanding. She must have immediate gratification, often lacks patience, will rage over the most insignificant events, and will overreact to people and situations that would not bother most of us. For her, the only constant is her inconstancy. You never know where you stand with her. One minute she loves you, the next, she hates you. There are no subtleties in her world.

The borderline engages in "splitting"; that is, she idealizes a person at one moment and in the next may utterly devalue him. All depends on her perception at the time. For the borderline, personal history and situational context hold no meaning and provide no nuance. You are either her friend or her foe, good or bad, right or wrong. While we see shades of grey, allowing us emotional flexibility, the borderline's palette is limited to black and white. If you are not *with* the borderline, you are *against* her, and you will suffer her fury. Where we would restrain our impulses and emotions, the borderline will lash out with no concern for decorum. Ranting, raving, and raging (including physical quarrels marked by slapping, punching, and hitting) are natural modes of communication for her. Moreover, a borderline is more likely than any other type to exhibit episodes of self-mutilation or suicidal behavior.

In case I'm not getting the borderline personality disorder profile across clearly, let me ask if the name "Alex Forrest" rings any bells for you. Alex Forrest is the borderline other woman character played to perfection by Glenn Close in the 1987 thriller and cautionary tale, *Fatal Attraction*. Alex, the borderline extraordinaire, exhibits nearly all classical symptoms. She is unstable, volatile, chaotic; reckless and lacking impulse control. She swings between adoring and then devaluing the object of her alternating love and hate. She is needy, anxious, depressed, and fearful of abandonment, feeling unworthy one moment, then entitled the next. She knows no personal boundaries, is prone to self-mutilation and suicidal ideation, and has sudden, severe mood swings and promiscuous sexuality. She is punishing (which can include violent conduct—though not typically murder) when her needs aren't immediately met.

Recent statistics tell us that 2 percent of the population suffers from borderline personality disorder and most are women—approximately 75 percent or so. Though many adolescents exhibit borderline tendencies, most professionals will not diagnose an individual until she is past age eighteen, as personalities are still forming through the late teen years. Interestingly, studies reveal that a large percentage of borderlines have suffered some kind of abuse (sexual, psychological, or physical) or neglect as children and that most have an insecure, anxious/ambivalent attachment style.

No matter how one comes to have borderline personality disorder, as a group, they are remarkably similar in their inability to control their overwhelming emotions. Paradoxically, a borderline's general inability to moderate her extreme feelings and reactions eventually provokes others to react negatively and, ultimately, abandon her, which is her ultimate fear.

The classic borderline interloper is unpredictable, treacherous, and often self-destructive. She acts this way due to an underlying identity disturbance, meaning she has no real sense of what makes her tick. While most of us have a pretty good idea of what and who we are and how we function, this is not true for the borderline. Her crucial lack of self-understanding causes her to suffer deep depression and chronic fears of abandonment, which she tries to cover with bravado and arrogance. Within the borderline personality disorder is a sad, threatened, frightened human who is struggling to hide it all. What you see on the surface is very different from what is inside, especially if she's looking to sink her hooks in your husband.

Why would your husband even bother with this impossible creature of chaos? Because while the borderline personality disorder woman is ensnaring her victim—your husband—she's able to be charming and mysterious, not to mention highly and often inappropriately sexual. Accustomed to covering their core emptiness, many borderlines are experts at making a person feel like he's the center of the universe. More than seductive, borderlines can be cunning and manipulative and are expert at finding someone who will take care of them. They appeal to the savior instinct (to rescue the weak, help the downtrodden) in some men. That's how they get their pedicured foot in the door to your decent, kind husband's life. When a borderline combines her mate-pleasing qualities with her impulsive and reckless sexual activity, she can become nearly irresistible. If your mate succumbs, the borderline other woman will be ever so appreciative and will show him just how grateful she is by performing fellatio on him under his desk, while he's talking on the phone with a colleague or, most perfidious of all, *you!*

For all these reasons, the first few months of an affair with a borderline damsel in distress with an insatiable libido can be downright intoxicating—how fun, how wild, how outrageously erotic, how dangerous. (Recall the *Fatal Attraction* scenes where Dan Gallagher, Michael Douglas's character—a married man, lawyer, dad, and unfaithful husband—fornicates with Alex all over the place?) The liaison can seem almost like a religious experience.

Remember, it's the borderline's full-time job to hook up with a person who'll prevent her deep-seated feelings of emptiness and abandonment from surfacing. To do this she will keep her lover very busy with her turmoil, which *can* captivate at first. So, if your husband's been straight-laced and fun-starved, beware! As the borderline other woman lacks boundaries, she might be so bold as to enlist you, the wife, in her husband-snatching endeavor—unbeknownst to you, of course. Accordingly, be on red alert if a woman seems want to manipulate you into getting information about or closer to your husband.

Antisocials

Most people really have a hard time understanding the antisocial personality disorder, as most mental-health professionals today call it. This is the behavior that tabloids and television series seem inclined to label with terms like "sociopath" or the older clinical tag, "psychopath." People with antisocial personality disorder are not psychotic (they know reality from fantasy and right from wrong), but they live purely by what Freud called the id. The id represents our unconscious drive to fulfill primitive, instinctual urges, like instant gratification concerning food, sex, and domination over whatever we want. Think of the id as the devil on your shoulder, telling you "If you want it, take it."

A person with antisocial personality disorder has little to no filter on her id. Consequently, she only listens to the devil on her shoulder telling her to go ahead, do it. She will sleep with your husband, son, and father, and all on the same night, if it makes her feel good. She has no conscience and no empathy, and she will lie, cheat, steal—do anything it takes—to satisfy whatever urge she happens to have at the time. According to the American Psychiatric Association, about 3 percent of the male and 1 percent of the female population have ASPD. The antisocial person is generally incapable of loving, but may be exceptionally skilled at lovemaking.

People with ASPD know fact from fiction and right from wrong; they simply don't give a damn. They suffer no shame, guilt, regret, or angst. Antisocials show poor judgment, lack insight into self and others (which requires reflection and empathy), and fail to learn from experience. Though utterly unburdened by scruples, your basic interloper with antisocial personality disorder can be attractive, intelligent, and charming. You can find her in as many of society's high places as its low. Lacking any anxiety, she presents an image of cool, clear, calmness with nerves of steel. She can be bold and brash or quiet and reserved, whatever will work for her at the time.

So you have a fearless rival after your man—what happens next? She will aggressively pursue him, often by manipulation. If that technique fails, she might try intimidation, extortion, or worse. Whatever it takes, she will do it, or manipulate someone else to do it for her. Unlike the highly anxious borderline, the antisocial other woman lacks anxiety (a key factor in diagnosing which of the personality disorders you are working with). Often, she has a radar-like ability to hone in on others' vulnerabilities, giving her an inside track to your husband's psyche without ever seeming invasive or nosey.

Generally, your antisocial marital trespasser is charming and shrewd and will enter your husband's life with utter ease. That fun demeanor changes, however, if she doesn't get her way. Borrowing Congreve's line from *The Mourning Bride*, hell hath no fury like an unhappy or thwarted antisocial woman. She will do anything to meet her objectives, including breaking the law. We know a great deal about the person with antisocial personality disorder because many are found in prisons, where researchers can study their attitudes and behaviors. Naturally, the really good ones are never caught as they manipulate or talk their way out of trouble. Take a look at the scales used to assess the antisocial.

Do you remember the Long Island Lolita, Amy Fisher, who shot her lover's wife in the face? This could be your future if your husband hooks up with someone with an antisocial personality disorder.

Psychotic Dangers

Speaking of shooting the wife in the face, bad as she was, Amy Fisher was not psychotic. She knew exactly what she was doing and paid the price with a jail term. And while they can be cold-hearted, most antisocial women will not be out to kill you, though you should be on guard for their typically aggressive behavior, marked by lying, cheating, and stealing. Contrary to the neurotic with a personality disorder—who can function and recognize reality—the psychotic cannot do either.

Here are the danger signs for psychosis: delusions, hallucinations, violent behavior, disorganized speech (bizarre, often incoherent, talk), obsessive or compulsive rituals, and exceedingly disorganized or catatonic behavior (lasting more than a day and not caused by medications or drugs). Thankfully, psychosis affects less than 1.5 percent of the U.S. population and appears more often among males than females. Consequently, chances are good that your spouse would not knowingly become involved with anyone this sick. The danger lies when a borderline—or anyone else—leaves reality for the false world of delusions or hallucinations.

Psychopathic Personality Inventory

The higher a person scores on each of the following subscales, the more deeply embedded her antisocial personality disorder traits:

Impulsive nonconformity: Recklessness, rebelliousness, and unconventionality

Blame externalization: Tendency to rationalize one's bad behavior or blame others

Machiavellian egocentricity: Aggressive, selfish, and manipulative conduct

Carefree nonplanfulness: Failure to plan or think ahead

Stress immunity: Suffers no, low, or little anxiety

Social potency: The power to control or influence others

Fearlessness: Readiness to take risks without concern for outcomes

Cold-heartedness and lack of sentimentality: Unresponsiveness to others' suffering

If your husband is involved with a person who has lost her grip on reality, you and your children might require protection. You can try to have the person committed to a mental institution or arrested, depending upon the level of danger or threat. In the meantime, tell your local authorities and consider installing a security system.

CHAPTER 5

Where Temptation Waits

Now that you know who the marital interloper is and how she thinks—about herself, your partner, and perhaps even you (if she considers you at all)—this chapter will explore the places where she lays in wait and poaching abounds.

Promoting a continuing, intimate connection to your husband is the best way to disincline him from seeking companionship, encouragement, or even sex outside your union. Unfortunately, sometimes more is needed to protect your marriage from the predators who, given the chance—or opportunity—would tear your wedded world asunder.

The phrase "like a kid in a candy store" can apply to a number of environments many husbands find themselves in today, where numerous women will go after any man they want, disregarding his marital or relationship status and regardless of the consequences. To maximize your chances of retaining your mate's enduring, undivided devotion, you must address the predictable threats that arise under certain well-documented, marriage-hostile conditions.

Though a potential mate-stealer can approach your husband anywhere, some sites are notoriously more troublesome than others. The marital interloper knows she has better odds for success at these hot spots due to several physical factors: your absence, her presence, and your husband's unwitting good nature, or his initially innocent willingness to help her out or to simply listen to her tales of heartache and woe or stories of frolic and fun.

Lucky for you, those very aspects that make certain places so conducive to affairs are exactly the same features that allow you, the wife, to prevent any budding relationship from taking permanent, damaging hold. When it comes to mate-poaching, you'll see that it's mostly about her lack of boundaries, access to your husband—and a possible personality disorder—mixed with your mate's unmet needs, an innate desire for variety, and some old-fashioned testosterone.

Whether it's at work, worship, shopping, or play, temptations are abundantly available. If you are aware of the dangers that exist, you and your partner can make a plan or a pact as to how he should deal with the inevitable flirters that lurk outside your marital bond. It's time to take a look at the most common danger zones, discuss why they are marital hazards of the first degree, and determine what you, as a wife, should know and do when your husband is out of your sight—and possibly in someone else's.

Employment Opportunities

Many researchers have confirmed the workplace is a hotbed of human attraction and extramarital affairs. Many a professional woman has sacrificed her youth to concentrate on her career, and there comes a time when some of these women are satisfied with their professional development and decide it's time to find a mate. So there these women are, single, divorced, or even unhappily married, and they see your husband. They already have work in common; perhaps they share another interest?

There's no downside to prevent the woman from engaging in a little nonverbal flirting to see where it goes.

Why is the workplace fraught with infidelity? There's the obvious fact: that familiarity (or the propinquity effect, described on page 45) can be a serious force at play when a woman at work sets her sights on your husband.

Then, there is the fact that younger women (under the age of thirty-five) are often more open to certain sexual acts (such as oral and anal sex) and could use this willingness to lure your husband.

Perhaps most dangerous of all from a psychological perspective is that the office represents a microcosm of the family. Both the potential interloper and your husband feel comfortable and depend on one another. Access is open, and depending upon their relationship, boundaries can be low or nonexistent. Besides, there are the long hours and shared projects, deadlines, and accomplishments that stimulate the same physiological systems as those that become aroused when someone falls in love. In addition to the sensations of desire and longing caused by a release of the neurotransmitters and hormones of attraction, the employment environment itself can promote these transitory, yet potent, passionate impulses by sponsoring compulsory social events that feature fun and exclude family and spouses.

Employment atmospheres that exclude spouses but are friendly to colleagues place the potential mate-poacher alone with your husband in familiar, positive surroundings. All it

| Where the Girls Are | Over twenty years ago, sociologist Laurel Richardson wrote that women held two out of every five executive or management positions. Today, women's presence in the work force has grown at all levels, from intern to CEO. |

takes is one step over the line for an unholy alliance to form between your working spouse and his coworker (or subordinate, boss, or client), sealed with a secret kiss that could doom both careers if the confidence is broken. You are now the odd man out of your own marriage.

As far as affairs and infidelity are concerned, researchers have found that all workplaces are not created equal. Settings that involve touching others (colleagues, customers, patients, or clients), sharing personal disclosures, or spending time alone with others provide more opportunity for extramarital play with someone work-connected. The more touch, private time, and personal disclosure there is on the job, the more you are replicating the same dynamics that are at work (literally) when people socialize, get to know one another, and become fond of each other. Recall how self-disclosure and exclusiveness breed intimacy in a couple. Privacy leads to secrecy and a common bond, and human touch cements affection and fondness.

Consider what happened to Kevin, an honorable religious family man. A trim, ruggedly handsome forty-five-year-old dentist, Kevin enjoyed a successful practice where he employed two assistants and three hygienists. His wife, Gerri, would come in to do billing when necessary. Kevin's office was a

One Woman's Affair of State

"It started because we were, I suppose, healthy, handsome people in very pressurized jobs. I think what was happening was we were both going home to an empty flat. Sooner or later you start chatting and sharing confidences and, like you say, come home with me—and he did." —Edwina Currie, House of Commons, on her affair with former British Prime Minister John Major pleasant, upbeat place to work, including many social activities planned for the staff. Kevin adored Gerri and their kids and would never do anything to jeopardize his family life.

Kevin hired a twenty-three-year-old assistant, Ann, who was well qualified and very well built. The fact that she had an outstanding body posed no problem for Kevin for the first six months. Then, whenever Ann was assisting Kevin, she would lean over so he could feel her breast (just barely). Each time she did this, Kevin would move away.

Next, Ann began staying at work after office hours to "learn all she could from him." At every opportunity, Ann would stroke Kevin's ego, and he enjoyed her attention. He noticed that when they all went to the regularly scheduled office luncheons, Ann always sat next to him, even when his wife was present, sitting on the other side. During one staff luncheon, Kevin felt a slight pressure on his thigh. He realized it was Ann's hand on his leg; Gerri didn't notice a thing. Kevin didn't move his leg away. He felt excited to have this woman wanting him, with his wife right there.

That luncheon launched Kevin's marital crisis. The next day at work, Ann believed that she had tacit approval to go further with Kevin. Ann left work with the other staff at closing time, only to return, knowing that Kevin would still be there. Kevin wasn't sure if he was happy or angry to see her. He asked her to go and have a seat in his office. When Kevin entered, he found Ann reclining on his couch with her top off. He told me that at this point he had an obvious erection. He and Ann proceeded to do everything he ever dreamed of doing with her, save sexual intercourse.

Kevin was mortified when he explained how he felt "defiled by his hormones and lack of control." That night, when he returned home, Gerri was waiting for him with a snack and some good conversation. Kevin suffered a panic attack so severe that Gerri wanted to call the rescue squad. Kevin told her that he needed rest and if he didn't feel better, he'd get help. (That was when he made the appointment to see me.)

After much discussion, Kevin had a plan to save his marriage. Realizing that he gave in to temptation, and that he didn't want to be tempted again, he resolved to decrease his staff, letting the last hire go first. He only prayed that Ann would not claim he sexually harassed her or worse, from Kevin's point of view, tell Gerri what had happened between them that one night. (He had no intention of sharing these events with Gerri, ever.) Kevin informed Ann that he'd have to let her go and gave her what amounted to "a golden parachute" (a guaranteed termination payment, regardless of work performance, unheard of in the dental hygienist trade) to leave his office. He also paid her health insurance premiums until she found another job.

Ann took a four-month vacation before she sought a new position. Kevin knew he had been had by this busty young operator and learned from this experience. Kevin remains a happily married man, keeps his office staff at more then an arm's length away, and has asked Gerri to join him on all staff hiring positions from now on, just in case.

Stopping Trouble Before It Starts

In the example of Gerri and Kevin, Gerri was not able to identify Ann, the seductress, as a clear and present danger to her marriage, but she was. If she'd read this book, Gerri would have known enough to question why her husband should hire a great-looking, young, relatively inexperienced dental assistant when a more ordinary-looking experienced worker would do just as well, if not better, for the office.

Also, aware that mate-poaching happens regularly, Gerri would have been sure to determine Ann's personal level of interest in her husband. This way Gerri could have determined whether the new office bombshell wanted more than just a strictly career-based, professional office rapport with Kevin. Aware of the risks that someone like Ann might bring to the office, Gerri would have known to ask Ann, why she, a dental assistant, was making a point to be with Kevin in ways and manners that the other staff did not—sitting next to him at luncheons and staying after hours at the office with Kevin but without patients or pay.

Aware that mate-guarding is her right and her duty, Gerri would have employed whatever strategies she needed to protect her relationship. Her strategies might have included drawing firm boundaries between the staff and her husband, ensuring no special access and no special privileges. While not every wife has this kind of opportunity for input (okay, control), it's your prerogative to take full advantage of every advantage you have.

Even if you can't control your man's work environment or colleagues, there are things you can do and situations you ignore at your marital peril. The following fact patterns should provoke your active interest:

1. Watch out for allotted time with one particular person that becomes a pattern and secret delight. The propinquity effect is not your friend in this situation. Secrets are trouble, and crushes can be impossible to cure when there's continuing, stimulating contact. Private lunches, after-work drinks and dinners, and special, secret meetings or phone calls of any kind are a no-no.

2. Your husband should not be keeping his feelings secret. Remember, a marriage requires trust and open constructive communication. If your husband finds himself attracted to a coworker, encourage him to discuss it with you. Help him find out what's happening and why, and fix it. (If you need a marriage counselor, fine.) In the meantime, he should

eliminate all nonprofessional contact with the person. He'll get over the attraction, and she'll move on to richer soil with a less vigilant wife.

3. Traveling or being alone with an attractive alternate is another potentially dangerous situation. Encourage your mate to make other arrangements and accommodations. Don't encourage him to be at the office after hours or on weekends when she's there and no one else is. If traveling on business together is necessary, arrange different flights and different hotels if possible. If your husband must travel with female colleagues, he shouldn't dine alone with them—a group is usually okay. There should be no private drinks in dark bars or meetings in hotel rooms. Have him give you and the kids a way to reach him whenever you want when he's away or at the office.

4. Make sure he has family photos to display in his office or to bring along on trips. A tattoo on his privates is optional.

WHAT YOU MUST DO:

1. Keep your lines of communication open and don't punish him for sharing temptations. You want him talking about his feelings and impulses. Use them to your advantage and to maintain intimacy (remember self-disclosure and sharing?) and relationship satisfaction. (See item ten on this list.)

2. Keep your eyes open and mind your man's feelings, thoughts, and actions. Remember, the best defense is a good offense. Stay proactive when protecting your husband from the amoral women of the world who couldn't care less how much havoc they wreak in the lives of others.

3. Show up at your husband's office for lunchtime surprises (of all kinds—use your imagination and perhaps a long rain-. coat and heels), and be sure to demonstrate your affection

for him in an acceptable but clear way by using what the experts call "tie signs"—holding hands, a hug, a kiss, or a tender stroke on the cheek—to make sure that everyone is aware that you and your husband are permanently bonded. Perhaps you have pet names, a private language, inside jokes, or other signs of insular coupledom? Use them, too. Leave no room for doubt that you are his life mate, his *wife*. Cast a cold, warning eye on those who would set their sights on your husband. They will pass by.

4. Plaster your man's work area with family photos: you and him; you, him, and the kids (if you don't have any, rent some for the photos); you, him, his parents, and the kids; you, him, and your parents and the kids; you, him, all of your parents, and the kids, the dogs, the cats, and the like. The visual message you're sending to the would-be at-work poacher is "You wanna try to break this up?" In many instances, she'll see that you and your husband are part of a united family front that she cannot penetrate—though this tack won't always dissuade a poacher with a bad attitude and a personality disorder.

5. Give your husband a beautiful framed portrait (professionally done, if you want) of you for his desk. Get a wallet-size copy for him to carry—at all times.

6. Make sure he wears a wedding band at work. If he loses the original, buy a cheapie one at Costco till he can replace it. If he's at a job where he can't wear a ring for safety reasons, buy him a chain so he can wear it around his neck.

7. One of the most infamous lovers of all time, Heloise, wrote famously passionate, erotic letters to her lover and secret husband, Abelard. Try your hand at remembering fondly the "lewd visions of the pleasures" you shared with your husband and see if it doesn't help keep his love alive and exclusively yours.

8. Keep in touch by phone; nothing else is like hearing each other's voice. Or, put an e-note into his pants or vest pocket via text message through his cell phone or PDA. As for content, cute is good, funny is fine, sexy is top of the list. For a list of common text acronyms with definitions, go online to *www.sharpened.net.*

9. Attend as many of your husband's company's functions as possible, and accompany your husband on as many business trips as you can. If you cannot attend, plant secret cards, letters, photos, or any erotic material (that you both enjoy and are comfortable with) in his travel bag or shaving kit. Know where he'll be going, staying, eating, and ask him to call at night. Devote time to him over the phone, meet his emotional needs, and make him pine for you.

10. Include fantasy, arousal, and novelty in your sex life. You are glad he's free enough and secure enough to share his thoughts and urges without fear of your wrath or punishment. Recall that men are visually stimulated and geared for variety—at least in their mind. If he's got a crush, let her image pump his mental tires while you ride the, um, bicycle, gaining the benefit of his love and attachment-inducing sex hormones, vasopressin and oxytocin.

In the meantime, review these mate-retention tactics:

- **Vigilance:** Keep your eyes and ears open and listen to your alarm bells of warning.
- **Concealment of mate:** Keep him at home, or dress him like a happily married guy. Some say making him fat and happy is helpful, though it's not healthy, so I can't recommend it.

- **Monopolization of time:** Make a busy life together. How could he have an affair when you have him scheduled for family fun and frolic during every free hour?
- **Jealousy induction:** Make him feel what's good for the guy is good for the girl. Flirt and let him see you still attract the boys—or men.
- **Infidelity punishment:** Let him know the consequences of infidelity are divorce, loss of half of his assets, isolation, ignominy, opprobrium, and regret.
- **Emotional manipulation:** Make him feel that you are his only worthy love object.
- **Commitment manipulation:** Do what you must to make him invest in you and your relationship.
- **Derogation of competitors:** Diss your rival.
- **Resource display:** Let your guy know that you're a good catch.
- **Sexual inducements:** Does this need explanation?
- **Appearance enhancement:** Make yourself look great and feel great.
- **Loving and caring:** Nothing is better than devotion and tenderness at home.
- **Verbal possession signals:** He's mine, as in "my husband, my husband, my husband."
- **Physical possession signals:** Try hand holding, cuddling, maybe even handcuffs.
- **Possessive ornamentation:** A wedding band should say it all.

Appendix D includes a full version of the Mate Retention Inventory; though this is not a scored test, you can answer the questions there to assess your style of guarding your mate and marriage.

Employ the mate-guarding strategies that fit your tempera-
ment and context (be mindful of the law and good sense). Let
your husband know by your actions and words that all he needs
is you, while alerting your rival she's picked the wrong guy and
girl to mess with.

Marital Travel Advisory

Working men often have to travel on business. A husband's solo
travel plans can bring many a solid couple to the brink of a big-
time argument, particularly if women from work are scheduled
to attend. Even when the travel pals are not female, the places
businessmen patronize, whether for business or pleasure, are
full of grown-ups away from home and free from their daily
responsibilities and ties that bind.

When a husband hits the road and is off to the airport—
with its bars and private airline clubs—a wife could make herself sick with worry contemplating the opportunity that awaits
him: drinks, a lively exchange, or perhaps a cross-continent chat
with an attractive stranger in the semi-private, dimly lighted,
comfy business class cabin. And if sharing a blanket and some
booze over a long flight isn't a scary image for a spouse, how
about those hotels and gyms, sporting events, or "guy vacations"
that commence in earnest once your guy deplanes and exits the
airport? What can a wife do to counteract the strong pull of
"what happens in Vegas stays in Vegas," where he can almost
feel the marital vows straining under the weight of ubiquitous
temptation?

It never hurts to occasionally remind your mate of the consequences of infidelity. One of my patients tells her husband
that she has a friend, family member, or colleague wherever
he travels. This way, he always feels there's always a possibility
of bumping into someone connected to his wife. She has also,
on occasion, visited her spouse unannounced as a surprise. He

never knows when that will happen. Feel free to develop your own mate-protection mechanisms by using your imagination and the list of tactics from page 82.

Let's Get Physical Fitness Center

Gyms, health clubs, and spas are where the buff gather to roam around in skin-tight spandex to pump iron, flatten abs, and sometimes to do so much more. Because going to the gym involves hours of time away from home and family, it's been a common alibi for men having affairs for many years. It's time alone in the presence of many other scantily clad, well-toned, body-conscious adults. Plus, gyms have showers (great for washing away the evidence of adultery), lockers (useful to hide clothes, love letters, sex toys), and often a bar or small café (to lubricate the events that follow).

Why would any wife want her husband in the center of temptation and barbells? You wouldn't, but here's how to handle your husband's workout routine. Get him a membership to the best all-male gym or club you can afford. Make it something special and give it as a gift. Consider a beautiful facility in your area that's like the Union Club in Manhattan, an exclusive, all-male sanctuary with amenities he'd enjoy: a bar, restaurant, library, and hotel. He'll love it and so will you. You might also join a gym together and get all sweaty and naked afterwards.

You can also establish other exercise routines together. Go for a walk, weather permitting. My daughter and her pilot husband set aside forty-five minutes each evening when he's not traveling to walk three miles while they listen to their favorite NPR programs and discuss the matters of the day. Taking up a sport or hobby together is good as well, as long as you don't get too competitive. Try tennis, golf, sailing, hiking, or any number of the other activities that allow you to share experiences.

Make friends with more happily married couples and deepen your bond as you elevate your fitness, fun, and health.

Home: The Danger Zone

The next danger area is your home. Some home workers (babysitters, nannies, and au pairs) can be more of a potential danger to a marriage than any other brand of interloper. These familiar faces can give the phrase "trading spaces" a new, quite literal, meaning. The danger lies in their access to the inner sanctum—your home—and the fact that they are privy to the emotional overtones of everyone in the household, particularly you and your husband. These women, who are often young teens without their own parental authority figures present, have the opportunity to be at home with your spouse when you are not present, giving them unlimited, unquestioned access to your man and your family on very familiar, informal territory. Do you remember how the late Michael Kennedy was nearly prosecuted for statutory rape after his then wife, Vicki Gifford

Nannies That Made the Leap

Wives who were once home workers include Marsha Garces, Robin William's current wife; Kimberly Driscoll, Joe Piscopo's current wife; and the wondrous Wendi Deng, media mogul, Rupert Murdoch's current wife. Young Wendi's first husband, Jerry Cherry, was the forty-plus father of the Californian family that sponsored Wendi and invited her to live with them in the States. Mrs. Cherry filed for divorce after finding photos her husband had of Wendi in a hotel room. Jake and Wendi didn't last long as a married couple. Five months into their marriage, Wendi had moved on to the next man.

Kennedy, discovered he had been having a affair with his kids' very underage babysitter in plain sight of everyone in cozy Cohasset, Massachusetts?

To avoid ouster by the nanny, you must be comfortable setting and maintaining boundaries to protect your turf, your husband, and ultimately, control of your home. Who you hire will be a test of your good judgment. Make your selection first by qualifications, and then consider your panoply of mate-protection tactics (oversight, control, denigration—of her "traits" or "talents"—and limits). Considering the socially and legally acceptable means setting firm boundaries, such as, "If you sunbath nude around the pool you will be fired and sent back to your parents." If you are on a diet, it is not a great idea to go to a candy store. Why place your husband in a situation in his own home where he may have to fight impulses on a daily basis? And, from the other perspective, consider the nanny who is motivated to find a home (yours) or a green card.

If your husband has always had a thing for blondes and never was attracted to redheads, yup, redhead it is. If she is pear shaped and needs dental work, better yet. If she has thick ankles and that is not his preference, she is the girl, and so it goes. Remember how your mom told you that it's just as easy to love a rich boy as a poor one? In this instance, it's even better to hire a plain girl than a beauty. Still, be careful out there. Looks aren't everything, and conniving poachers come in all flavors. Finally, though they have less access, the same principles apply to daytime cleaning ladies, occasional babysitters, and the like.

One of my patients, Helen, hired a young woman, Toni, who was earning money to pay her tuition for graduate school by cleaning houses. She was recommended by a friend who said she was the only cleaning person her husband never complained about and she did a great job. Helen hired Toni sight unseen based on the recommendation. Her friend neglected to mention that Toni was tall, fit, and very bright. Helen was secure, but she was still slightly uncomfortable with the degree of friendliness that ensued between her husband and this comely young housekeeper, who was studying math. In short order, Helen's husband, a scientist who loved math, had offered to tutor Toni. A cozy relationship began to develop between them, and Helen immediately fired Toni, switching instead to a cleaning service. Helen never confronted her husband about the girl but said that the cleaning company would be more efficient—with five people, they'd be in and out of the house within an hour.

When Toni called Helen's house a number of times to seek tutoring from her husband, Helen told her that he wasn't available and suggested, politely, that she not call again. Three months later, the original friend who had recommended Toni was separated from her husband. He was now living with Toni.

Moral of this story: Just as you take care not to leave your valuable jewelry or cash out for someone to steal, don't give your husband less care and vigilance than you would a watch or hundred-dollar bill.

The Internet—A Modem to His Heart

The last infidelity danger to deal with is the poacher who sits at the other end of the Internet connection. She could live next door or around the world. Due to the electronic architecture of the World Wide Web, it makes virtually no difference. The Internet allows her secret access to your man wherever he may be: at work, in a public space, an automobile, an aircraft, a dentist's office, or even sitting at home before the bluish glow of the family PC. Whether she prefers communicating through chat rooms, e-mail, instant messaging, or video-conferencing via Webcams, all your potential rival needs to cyber-touch your mate is a PDA, a computer, or cell phone and she's good to go. Given all this technology, what's a wife to do?

First, let's define the issue. We're not addressing the more general problem some men have with cybersex. Here, we are focusing on the situation in which a specific woman is after your husband and uses the computer to communicate with him. Let's clarify the distinction.

Cybersex often involves a nonspecific, generic desire on the part of the computer user (the cybersexual) to use the Internet to gratify his sexual needs by viewing assorted pornographic photographs or interactive, live sex shows or by participating in triple-X chat rooms. Unless you condone or participate in these activities, a cybersex habit usually harms a marriage by causing sexual estrangement between the couple, as well as secrecy and shame on the part of the participant.

This habit does not, however, regularly lead to a face-to-face meeting with a real person. (Few Internet porn models make house calls.) So, while you do have a problem if your husband is addicted to Internet porn or partakes of cybersex (seeking

Cyber Snooping

Though ill-advised and illegal (interfering with someone's mail, even if it's electronic, violates state and federal laws), if you want to know what's going on inside your husband's computer, never mind his head, there are ways to investigate. Your options include things like PC Pandora, online at *www.pcpandora.com*. (Doesn't the name say it all?) But beware: You run the risk of prosecution and civil sanctions if you interfere with someone's mail—ordinary or electronic. (See more in Chapter 13.) Proceed at your peril.

porn or sexy chat via computer for stimulation, and then, masturbating to reach climax before the time of the session is over), it's not the same problem as when a certain someone is after your man—or vice versa.

Most people with Internet porn addictions need personal and professional intervention to help break them of their habit and wean them back to human-to-human contact with sexual boundaries and activities that are acceptable to the porn addict and his partner. Dr. Kimberly S. Young has been working with clients on the issue of cybersex and Internet addiction since the 1990s. Young has come up with the ACE Model, an interesting approach to deal with and heal the craving for sexual gratification via computer. The ACE Model is based upon the characteristics of the compulsive behavior that makes it resistant to treatment, self-control, and containment, as follows:

The "A" stands for anonymity. Computers provide a mantle of invisibility allowing a person virtual (forgive the pun) impunity for actions that would be deemed totally unacceptable by most of the people in his intimate circle.

The "C" stands for convenience. Due to the near ubiquity of the Internet, the privacy of delivery, and overabundance of available pornographic content, sex is literally available to anyone, anytime, anywhere.

The "E" stands for escape. The pursuit and ultimate satisfaction of the urge for cybersex provides a person with tension relief (by satisfying the compulsion to seek sex on the Internet), as well as a reprieve from a person's "real life" identity, say from a socially inept, poorly equipped, prematurely ejaculating short, fat, bald, ugly guy—or anyone with poor self-esteem or untreated sexual or social dysfunction—into an instant Internet Lothario.

If, on the other hand, your husband is conducting a sexually charged, emotional affair over the Internet that is directed to a specific person and is building up to a face-to-face meeting, you are in a different situation. Not necessarily better, but different. Instead of dealing with a man who lusts for anonymous, autonomous sex, involving only himself and pornographic imagery, conducting an Internet affair with a specific human being who's motivated to make real contact (not perform for money) is much more similar to a real-life affair, but there are subtle differences between the two scenarios.

If your husband is electronically contacting a woman he's already met in the flesh, the e-mails he writes her are merely a quick, convenient means of computer courtship. They deepen their relationship by writing, but they have already made that physical connection (whether or not it's become sexual) in the real world. They've gazed into each other's eyes; heard the tones of the other's voice; experienced the cadence of the other's movements; read the nonverbal, visual cues and gestures; smelled each other's scent (some would say pheromones); and perhaps already felt the frisson of excitement from the other's touch. They have already hit it off. Their electronic correspondence keeps their spark alive till they meet again. In this case, you'll need to implement the mate-retention strategies you'll find in later chapters to end what your mate-guarding tactics did not prevent.

However, if you suspect that your husband is chatting with a person he's never met in real life but to whose persona he's taken an electronic shine, it's a totally different matter. First, both of them are in a fantasy land where each is able to carefully construct and edit the written material they send to each other. Their communications are devoid of the normal human nuances, cues, and context upon which real people have relied for millennia to gather information and to form judgments about others—at least until we got connected in the late last century.

Your cyber rival can present herself as whomever, whatever she wants to be, unfettered by the reality that bogs you, the wife, down in the real world. The computer-pal can seem witty, charming, alluring, and sexy after she's carefully composed her racy love notes to your husband. She can even alter her pictures so she looks like anyone or anything she wants. Who knows what she's really like in life? The same is true of your husband. He can literally invent himself as he composes each message. He might have presented himself as a single guy: no wife, no kids, no house, and no mortgage.

This unreal bubble of space allows both parties to fabricate any identities they want while they, paradoxically, self-disclose like crazy. In the process, their exchanges can grow profoundly more personal. As they pseudo-interact, they can become much more intimate, far faster than any socially acceptable real-life relationship could ever develop. Remember, anonymity, like drugs and alcohol, is a very powerful disinhibitor. What's more, this artificial, context-free communication often causes the man to project an image of the computer pal based upon his own desires. Generally, these projections cannot withstand the reality of a face-to-face meeting, particularly when the cyber lover is nothing like your man imagined her to be.

So, what do you do? First see the signs. You may note a distancing that hasn't existed before or less sexual activity, which may be the result of mutual masturbation while the cyber pair is online. You might notice changes in the phone bills or the fact that he may now want to pay the bills and you don't get to see them. You might see him spending less time with the family, or he might begin to wake up in the middle of the night to "watch television" (when he's really on the computer), and you notice that the cache on your computer's history bar is always clear in the morning. If you suspect he's up to no good, check his cookies and computer cache (where temporary Internet files are stored) and consider keeping an eye on the pulldown bar on Google or other search engines. (For help on tracking Web pages visited, go online to *http://help.stargate.net* and click the "Web browsers" link.) And of course, keep the lines of communication open about what you've found. Insist that the computer stay in a communal area and that use be reasonable: work, pleasure reading, research, games, and staying in touch with family and pro-marriage pals.

If you notice any of these or other suspicious behavior changes in your mate, you must address them—immediately—before he has the opportunity to form an alliance with his computer or any particular cyber chick. It is all about nipping this habit (whether general or specifically directed) in the bud, before it becomes a compulsion. If you haven't been attentive to these changes as they appeared, try talking to your husband. Throwing away the computer won't eliminate the problem. The healing process will involve work and usually therapy. It will take time to build trust again, once you have identified and resolved the issues in your marriage (or your mate) that led him to seek emotional comfort or sexual release (or both) from an inanimate object, when you were there in the flesh all the time.

Depending upon the facts, therapy can usually help. If the cybersexual's activity upsets both of you, a professional can help you communicate to figure out whose needs are not being met in the relationship or how to share fantasies in a way that does not threaten, harm, or shame anyone. Sometimes, weaning the cybersexual off the computer is difficult. But by replacing the destructive conduct with positive, reinforcing real-life activity (a willingness to explore new sensual ideas and a commitment to make sex a shared, marital matter), many couples are able to regain trust and intimacy and unplug from all cyber others.

CHAPTER 6

A Look in Your Marital Mirror

When you suspect that a marital trespasser is on the scene, you need to start out knowing where your rival lurks, and how she thinks, feels and acts. Your next step is to gain insight into your own behavior, beliefs, and worldview. What's more, you must reflect upon your type of marriage, even your kind of mate. As you'll learn, some kinds of men (narcissists, borderlines, sociopaths, criminals—think Scott Peterson—substance abusers, or risk takers) are difficult, if not downright undesirable or dangerous to have as husbands, while others are so sought-after that keeping them from falling into temptation presents a special challenge for the wife who is not a similar superstar. But before we begin analyzing you, your mate, and your marriage, let's take a look back to the days you first wed.

Your Positive Marriage Assortment

Your incentives to cement the relationship by marriage probably had much to do with finding someone of equal quality to you (just as attractive, ambitious, and philosophically suited) as it did with falling in love. Remember the discussion in Chapter 3 of how you choose your friends based on their similarity to you? Well, it's the same, only more so, when it comes to choosing a mate. Many researchers have confirmed that people pick their spouses according to how similar or compatible they are across a broad spectrum of traits. For instance, individuals commonly marry within a certain age group, religious affiliation, ethnicity, social standing, and even political mindset. Other important variables are intelligence, education, and even use of language and word choices. In all, people seem to select mates that are most like them: not far above or below them in rank and overall market value, if you will.

People tend to marry not too far up or down, and from an evolutionary standpoint this strategy makes sense. Marrying beneath you is not desirable because theoretically, at least, you could attract a mate at least as genetically and socially worthy as you are. Similarly, marrying too far above yourself (in resources, looks, intelligence, or social connections) doesn't work either. While you may be able to mate with those "superior" genes to gain offspring, chances are good that your partner will be poached by a superior rival, and you'll be left alone to fend for yourself and your kids—the worst that can happen, from a evolutionary aspect. Why bother to bring up this downer? If a trespasser is on the scene, or if she's threatening action, you must consider the status of your mate and the state of your marriage. For instance, if your mate has grown very successful or has in some way become distinguished, and you must consider the possibility that other women think that he's out of your league and potentially up for grabs. If your husband is loyal and in love, you don't have to worry. Unfortunately, his honor will not change the perceptions of the poachers who will give him a crack because that's what they do.

Once you've established your relationship, your best bet is to progress and grow as individuals over the duration of your relationship so you keep it fresh, exciting, interesting and equitable.

The Equitable Marriage

Equity theory is based on the concept that individuals want to maximize their outcomes—that is, they want to enjoy a high degree of benefit after taking cost and risk into account. Experts who study marriage have applied equity theory to intimate relationships to understand what happens when one of the couple feels that he or she is not getting a fair share, or, put another way, when one is giving more than one gets from the relationship.

Bear in mind that when we are talking about intimate relationships, the currency of equity or inequity is broader than what you'd expect in a group setting. With interpersonal relationships, the coin of the realm can be money, but it can also be personal services, affection, love, status, connections, potential, ambition, beauty, and so on. The bottom line is that individuals are happiest when they perceive themselves as being treated fairly.

If your husband feels likes he's not getting enough, or is being taken advantage of, he will begin to resent or be angry with his spouse—you—who is not giving him his due. He will begin to act out, while you may begin to feel guilty or depressed. Eventually, this imbalance in outcomes between spouses can cause severe dissatisfaction. At some point, the husband will begin to view available alternatives as more attractive than his wife, who is getting more than she's giving. Once that shift occurs, the husband's commitment to the marriage weakens. Depending upon the investment he's made in his marriage, he might just decide that he's out of there, that he can do better and be happier in a different and more equitable relationship.

What do you take from this section? First, that treating your mate fairly and equitably adds to his contentment and protects you from negative feelings, too. Plus, you don't have to be equal. He can make all the money, or vice versa, so long as you bring your special attributes to the table, such as giving him the affection and emotional support he needs. Whatever you two found in each other that made you special can continue to make you strong and successful as a married couple, as long as you're realistic.

If your rich, successful but homely husband married you because you had a body that could stop a clock and a face that could launch a thousands rockets, you should know that your beauty was an asset that you brought to the marriage. Of course you'll age and change, but your willingness to keep up appearances is probably still important to your mate. On the other hand, if your hubby was insecure and your nurturing way built his ego up to let him blossom, your worth to him is in the way you make him feel. He probably still counts on it, and any withholding on your part could make him feel cranky and unhappy.

Knowing Thyself—And Thy Husband

Equitable marriages are fine, but research reveals that the most important factor for predicting marital happiness (besides attachment style) is the personality of the husband and the wife. It's just that simple. The more positive, the more resilient, agreeable, and open you are, the more satisfaction you will find in your life and certainly your marriage. The same goes for your husband.

Let's consider the facts about personality and how it's assessed. Basically, our personality is the combination of how we see ourselves, our world, and our way in it. Our personality guides the way we think, perceive, feel, and act. Some psychologists approach the matter of personality by distinguishing stable characteristics from transitory phases ("traits versus states"). Here, we are interested in the traits that are more or less established once we reach adulthood, barring exceptional circumstances like extraordinary stress, serious illness, or misfortune. These catastrophic events can not only induce states that are uncharacteristic, but certain events, like the death of a child, can cause permanent psychological changes that affect what were thought of as that person's traits or personality. For our purposes, however, we will examine the issue of "personality" in the ordinary course.

In order to discuss personalities, we'll acquaint ourselves with the lingo of those who study personality traits for a living. Over the years, experts have identified five major domains of human functioning, known in intellectual circles as the Big Five: neuroticism, extraversion, openness, agreeableness, and conscientiousness. Shades of personality come from the facets, or subcategories, of these five domains. In combination, these traits describe the fullness of a person's thoughts, feelings, goals, actions, as well as his worldview of himself, and others:

Neuroticism
(emotional reactivity as opposed to emotional stability)

Anxiousness: Fear, worry for unknown cause; may be accompanied by physical signs and symptoms

Angry hostility: Emotional aggression or destructive behavior

Depressiveness: Sorrow or gloom

Self-consciousness: Introspection; an awareness of one's inner being (different from shyness, a social factor)

Impulsiveness: Inclination to act spontaneously, without considering the consequences of the action

Vulnerability: Susceptibility to injury, whether emotional or physical

Extraversion
(social power)

Warmth: Perception of degrees of kindness or affection

Gregariousness: Enjoyment of the company of others, sociable

Assertiveness: Self-assurance, inclined to act with confidence

Activity: The process of taking part in something, whether verbally, physically, or socially

Excitement seeking: Need to arouse or stimulate for self-gratification

Positive emotions: Sense of well-being marked by satisfaction

Openness
(intellectual and cultural; receptiveness to ideas, art, sensations)

Fantasy: Given to mental invention or whimsy

Aesthetics: The area of philosophy involved with various types of expression of beauty

Feelings: Ability to react to emotions

Actions: Movements, whether behavioral or physical, generally toward a goal

Ideas: Thoughts or conceptions produced or invented by the mind

Values: Principles or standards considered valuable; rules of life

AGREEABLENESS
(affection)

Trust: Complete confidence in another

Straightforwardness: Direct, not ambiguous

Altruism: Concern for the well-being of others, unselfish, giving

Compliance: Acquiescent; conceding to the will of others

Modesty: Conformance to the ultimate standards of the social setting or to the perceived propriety

Tendermindedness: Easily hurt or sensitive, fragile

CONSCIENTIOUSNESS
(work ethic)

Competence: Ability to care for one's self and make physical and emotional choices

Order: Logical system of emotional or social order or organization

Dutifulness: Inner need to meet obligations

Achievement striving: The need to accomplish or be successful; ambitious

Self-discipline: Control of one's conduct

Deliberation: Approach of a goal or issue with a firm, steady sense of commitment

In mentally healthy people, personality traits can be assessed through a test called the Revised NEO Personality Inventory (NEO-PI-R). For instance, in an assessment of the "neuroticism" domain, a person could encounter the following questions, each of which addresses the facets of that domain in order:

> *"I often worry that things may turn out badly."*
> *"I often get infuriated at the way people treat me."*
> *"Sometimes I feel I have no value."*
> *"In dealing with other people, I always dread making a social mistake."*
> *"I have trouble resisting my urges."*
> *"I often feel powerless and want someone else to solve my problems."*

Usually, the NEO-PI-R is scored by computer, and the results reveal a person's personal overall strengths (such as a positive view of life and willingness to consider other's points of view) and weaknesses (manipulativeness or inability to trust). You can take this test online at *www.personalitytest.net.* Read and follow the instructions and let your computer do the rest.

When you have your scores, ask your husband to take the test and share the results with you. If he needs convincing, tell him his scores will offer insight into how you can make your marriage more fulfilling (and allow you to keep a poacher at bay). If you don't succeed, try taking the test as if you were your husband and see if those scores don't ring true to the man you love. If you would like to take the real NEO-PI-R, you must contact a professional who has obtained the copyrighted test from Psychological Assessment Resources (PAR) and knows how to administer and score it.

Personality and Marital Satisfaction

What do the personality test results have to do with your marriage? According to the studies on marital satisfaction, quite a bit. One study that followed 300 Connecticut couples over fifty years (from the 1930s to 1980) showed the connection among marital stability, divorce, and spousal personality. In all, the researchers found that neuroticism (impaired emotional stability) of either the husband or wife contributes to marital trouble, but that other dynamics (social and environmental factors and liberal attitudes) are involved in the ultimate decision to divorce or remain married.

If you think your marriage suffers from someone's emotional instability, it's a good idea to see a professional to learn how to make things better before they get worse. If you or your spouse has emotional problems, treatment may help. The first step is to support the person with the problem and seek therapy. Unless you are involved with a true sociopath, you have the opportunity to at least explore the issues and find some remedy that will allow you to continue your marriage.

In addition to general emotional instability, or "neuroticism," there are three personality disorders that are known to

The "Big-Five" Hits the Big Time

The online dating site Eharmony.com has gone into the "marriage wellness" business. For a fee, couples can answer questions and get a lengthy computer-generated report based upon a range of typical psychometric dimensions of marital compatibility. The site does offer a freebie test to gain "five insights" into a marriage. Guess what those five insights are? You're right—they're the "Big Five" (except that neuroticism is called emotional stability).

make marriage difficult. You read about them in Chapter 3, which discussed what goes on inside many a predatory poacher's mind, allowing her to totally disregard your legal status as a wife and go after your husband anyway. If your husband happens to have one of these personality disorders, be prepared for challenges, heartbreak, and even danger down the road. Let's have a look.

Narcissistic Husbands

If your partner has a narcissistic personality disorder he will do whatever he must to make sure his needs for adoration, attention, and devotion are met by finding someone who will reflect his grandiose self-view back to him. If you, his wife, have tired of the job, he will find another to supply what he sorely needs. Given that the thirst for approval and affirmation is never slaked, it's impossible to satisfy the narcissist. As his wife, you are doomed to fail unless you can tolerate what most cannot, or unless your own personality lends itself to life with a narcissist.

Living with a narcissist means that your needs are never considered first and his drives and desires are paramount. Personality studies on the narcissistic population using the Big Five yield a general profile that's not too pretty. On the whole, narcissists are self-involved, lack concern for others, and are highly antagonistic. What's more, they are not generous, modest, or tenderminded. Narcissists score high marks for angry hostility (a neuroticism facet) and assertiveness (an extroversion facet). They are neither self-consciousness nor vulnerable, nor are they trusting, straightforward, or compliant. In other words, narcissists score low on all facets under the "agreeableness" domain. But that's not all. Narcissists are neither warm, nor excitement seeking (extroversion facets). They are not open to feelings, but do show openness to actions ("openness" facets), though those actions can be disturbing and hurtful.

Living with a narcissist is a full-time job. If you want to continue your relationship with this person, you know you'll be devoting a good part of your waking hours to meeting his needs, whatever they are and no matter what. It is akin to giving your life over to someone else. Are you willing to do this? If not, and a poacher comes along and tries to take him, you might consider yourself lucky. After the trauma, you might consider entering treatment to find out why you were attracted to a narcissist in the first place and, more important, why you remained. You don't want to make the same mistake again. Learn to get your needs met in a healthier way, in a functional relationship with a partner who'll consider what you want, as well as what he demands.

Borderline Mates

Recall the description of the poacher with borderline personality disorder. While it's similar for a man, only one in four people with this kind of personality disorder is male. According to the Big Five, your borderline husband will generally score very high under the neuroticism domain, particularly on the anxiousness, angry hostility, depressiveness, impulsiveness, and vulnerability facets. He might or might not be self-conscious, the only "neuroticism" facet that is not broadly characteristic of a person with borderline personality disorder. Borderlines have high scores under the feeling and action facets of the "openness" domain. Borderlines are controlled by their feelings, which change rapidly and with ferocity.

Unfortunately, borderlines can present another clinical challenge that can make life unbearable for a spouse: substance abuse. Just as certain personality disorders present problems in interpersonal relations, people prone to substance dependency or abuse can be just as tough to live with. Drug and alcohol abuse may cause changes in behavior that make the person almost unrecognizable. It also lowers normal inhibitions and boundaries, making fidelity particularly difficult to maintain. Unfortunately, borderlines often suffer from addictions caused by their attempts to self-medicate away the painful feelings associated with their underlying psychological issues. Feeling empty, fearing abandonment, and suffering from their own intense rages and mood swings, the borderline drives other people away—the precise outcome borderlines fear the most.

Though borderlines can be hypersexual, they are also extremely anxious (they have high scores under the "neuroticism" domain), yet they are less agreeable than others without their personality disorder. Therefore, according to what we know about divorce and personalities, your borderline husband might make you miserable, but chances are that he won't end the marriage by filing for divorce—that would be up to you.

The prognosis for borderlines can be good if they are willing to enter individual treatment and stay with the program. When their underlying issues (depression and anxiety) are addressed and managed, they gain relief from their distress, allowing a healthier way of living and relating to others, including a spouse.

But keep attuned to the situation. If you begin to see classic borderline symptoms returning (rapid mood changes, rages, withdrawal, isolation, or self-medication with drugs, booze, or food) seek help without delay. Proportionately, borderlines have a high suicide rate. Under their façade is an anxious, depressed person who may take the ultimate form of withdrawal to relieve his emotional pain. Therapy can help him understand his problems and teach him new tools to cope with his issues.

The Psychopath Husband

The person with an antisocial personality disorder—the proverbial "psychopath," as described in Chapter 4—is unencumbered by conscience and will do whatever he desires, with little or no thought to how others are affected. Given that information, you probably won't be surprised to learn that the person with anti-social personality disorder has a fairly scary personality profile marked by low agreeableness (low levels of self-discipline, duti-fulness, and deliberation, all facets of the "conscientiousness" domain), as well as remarkably low scores for self-conscious-ness and anxiety. This makes many of these people huge risk-takers and sometimes very successful entrepreneurs, athletes, and public speakers.

Similarly, sociopaths rate high marks for angry hostility, excitement seeking, and impulsiveness. As a whole, people with antisocial personality disorder make terrible life mates. You will always wonder if they are telling you the truth, or worse. Scott Peterson, convicted murderer of his pregnant wife, Laci, is by all accounts a sociopath. He didn't want her anymore, so he killed her. No problem for him, as he attempted to continue his affair with another woman (who thought he was a widower and who assisted the prosecution in its case against Scott). The mate with antisocial personality disorder is one you might want to send off to any poacher who will take him, with a farewell party—unless you have serious personality issues of your own.

Recognizing Your Weaknesses

We've reviewed the personality issues that could be giving your husband and you, not to mention your marriage, trouble. Hopefully, by now you've been able to get to a computer and take a Big Five–type test (if not the real thing) to gain feedback on where you stand on the personality continuum. While you might have received scores confirming that you are emotion-ally stable (low on the facets under the "neuroticism" domain), agreeable, open, conscientious, and socially adapt (ranking high under the "extroverted" facets), perhaps you didn't.

Here, we'll take a look at the personality profile of the proverbial long-suffering wife. If the description fits, you will gain the knowledge, and perhaps the motivation, to seek professional support so you can help yourself. Then, take a good hard look at whether your circumstances—your mate and your marriage—are worth protecting after all. Finally, after examining the typical personality traits associated with someone who remains in a masochistic relationship with a narcissist, borderline, or sociopath, we'll look at other mental coping mechanisms that can lead to marital mischief—or worse, the ultimate menacing presence of a mate-poacher.

Do You Court Disaster?

If you have a mate who falls into one of the troublesome trio (narcissist, borderline, or sociopath), you should consider whether your own personality traits have influenced your decision to enter and remain in a relationship with someone who is so difficult and in some cases, dangerous. Experts have also studied the traits of those who choose to partner with people who have the personality disorders we've addressed. If you're one of those people, you could have a dependent personality disorder. (There are more women with this disorder than there are men.)

Dependent personality disorder is present when a person exhibits a persistent and extreme need for others to take care of her, leading to fears of parting and passive, subservient behavior. Often, individuals with dependent personality disorder cling to people even if they are abusive, belligerent, or selfish. The symptoms can make it nearly impossible, and certainly challenging, for a person to leave a bad relationship and seek individual help. The classic Big Five traits of a person with dependent personality disorder are high scores for anxiousness, depressiveness, self-consciousness, and vulnerability (under the "neuroticism" domain); low assertiveness (under the "extraversion" domain); and, as you'd expect, very high scores under the compliancy, trust, and modesty facets (under the "agreeableness" domain).

If your Big Five scores fit the dependent personality profile, you now have sufficient information to assess whether your relationship is doing you more harm than good. You can also weigh the part you have played in setting up the circumstances under which your husband has taken advantage of you, possibly having affairs with others—perhaps with your implicit approval or passive disregard.

Review the following criteria for the dependent personality disorder diagnosis. Only a qualified professional can make a definite diagnosis. A person must exhibit five or more of these factors, which must have been present since early adulthood and cannot be the result of a recent trauma or actual threat of harm:

1. Requires a disproportionate amount of guidance and affirmation from others to make everyday decisions in life
2. Needs other people to control major areas of life and assume responsibility for them
3. Is unable to express disagreement with others, fearing loss of approval, support, or involvement
4. Lacks self-confidence in abilities or judgment (but not the energy or motivation); has trouble beginning projects or taking on matters for which she is held accountable
5. Will go to extremes (such as agreeing to do things that are unpleasant) to receive support, assurance, and care from others
6. Has amplified and irrational fears of being alone and is unable to care for self, causing feelings of distress and vulnerability when alone

7. When one relationship ends, instantly searches for a new relationship to provide support and nurturance
8. Is excessively worried about being left alone to care for self

If these factors hit home for you or someone you know, be aware that therapy can help ease the painful preoccupations and misconceptions that afflict a person with dependent personality disorder. In fact, psychotherapy is particularly helpful for these people because the psychotherapist can help the person understand where her assumptions about incompetence began, or at least to see how they affect her now.

Various methods (and when necessary, medications) are available to treat a person with dependent personality disorder, from cognitive behavioral therapy to a more classical analytic approach. This will help the person function as a competent adult with better coping and interpersonal skills. It will also help in neutralizing the fears and thoughts that shackle her to an unrewarding, frightened, passive life, particularly with another who is unkind, destructive, or downright dangerous.

Expect the Best

While you might not have a dependent personality disorder or even score high on dependent traits, your attitudes, behaviors, or beliefs could still be consciously or unconsciously setting the scene for your husband to fall into the arms of another. Consider the use of defense mechanisms, which are vital to protect the psyche from fearful or anxiety-inducing situations or to cope with circumstances that can be overwhelming. However, if they are overemployed, these protective mechanisms can distort a person's perceptions to such a degree that they become destructive, as opposed to temporarily helpful.

What are these ego defense mechanisms? According to Freud, most are unconscious and stem from repression or denial of reality that is too painful or disturbing to deal with. Anna Freud, Sigmund's daughter, took her dad's work a step further by cataloging many secondary ego defense mechanisms (such as displacement, fantasy formation, identification, projection, rationalization, reaction formation, regression, and sublimation). Still, most analysts agree that most ego defense mechanisms can be considered offshoots of repression or denial.

How do these defense mechanisms relate to you, a wife trying to protect her husband from the would-be marital trespassers in the world? The relationship could be very close. By their very nature, defense mechanisms distort or falsify the nature of the threatening, frightening, or anxiety-producing situation. Overuse of denial or rationalization can leave a wife vulnerable to circumstances that warrant immediate spousal intervention—like when your husband's assistant begins to buy him ties, or depends upon him for life advice. In order to exercise your wifely prerogative of vigilance and mate protection, you must be aware of (not in denial of, or rationalizing away) behavior that should be setting off your wifely alarm bells. Consider

Trimming the Clinging Vines

Remember reading about the psyches of your basic poacher-types in Chapter 4? The clinging vine type was mentioned in passing; but if your husband has become involved with one, watch out. If she is truly dependent, with a dependent personality disorder diagnosis, this woman will use her weaknesses to elicit help and sympathy from your husband. If he does not put an end to their relationship (sexual or not), she will continue to depend upon him for constant reassurance and attention. Once it's over, she'll replace him with another savior/protector.

a quote from Jacqueline Kennedy Onassis: "I don't think there are any men who are faithful to their wives." I can't think of a better example of a rationalization from a wife concerning her husband's extramarital affairs. If you use defense mechanisms to act as if you don't expect fidelity from your husband, you are almost assured not to receive it.

Just as interesting as the overuse of defense mechanisms is the possibility that a wife's conscious behavior and beliefs can set the stage for her husband's philandering. If, for instance, you learned from your earlier life experiences (such as a philandering father) not to expect fidelity from a husband, you can become an actor in your own self-fulfilling prophecy of marital infidelity. Here's how it works.

You hold a set of false beliefs about your husband. Communicating or acting on your false beliefs will elicit actions from him that will, eventually, bear out your initially false conceptions. So the next time you treat your husband like he's a cheating, no-good, down-and-dirty liar, he just might respond by confirming your worst fears. Why not, given that you've already judged him guilty?

A better strategy is to treat him with trust until he provides a reason to suspect wrongdoing, not the other way around. To

The Good News

Contrary to some researchers' work, who said that even happy marriages can be felled by infidelity, more recent research gives a different view. Unless the mate has a personality disorder, suffers from bipolar disorder (manic depression), or an ailment like a brain injury that derails his frontal lobe, where his conscience lies, people who are contented and in vital marriages tend to be protective of their bond.

put it another way, don't plant the seed of bad behavior yourself. There are plenty of poachers out there ready to make trouble without your paving their way for them with erroneous beliefs and defensive psychological processes.

Honoring Your Union

While no one and no couple is perfect, it's important to honor what's right between you as you work on what's wrong—or at least, what could stand improvement. Start by performing a simple marital-reality check and implement the lessons learned from this chapter. An equitable match is good; an uneven match is not as good. Likewise, agreeableness is good; neuroticism can be a challenge. Note the good things about your marriage as you become conscious of what leads toward martial satisfaction (warmth, affection, trust, and emotional stability) versus what makes a person want to run away (negative affect, emotional reactivity, poor communication, and high conflict).

In the meantime, never underestimate the power of positive reinforcement. We know from researchers that spouses are, like it or not, mutually reinforcing. This reinforcement can be positive or negative, depending upon the couple's pattern of interaction. Being aware of each other's personalities, strengths, and weaknesses can help you bring out the best in each other. Try expressing affection and gratitude to your mate for who he is, who he's become as a husband (and perhaps, father), and what he's accomplished during the marriage. Being inconsiderate and taking someone for granted corrodes a marriage by making a mate feel unappreciated and unloved. (This is a dangerous condition, especially in mind of Maslow's identification of human needs from page 11.) No matter what type or traits a person has, everyone likes to be acknowledged, just as they like attention and hearing the words "thank you" for the little things they do.

Part 3

SEIZING YOUR WIFELY
POWER

CHAPTER 7

Wifely Tricks and Advantages

Now you know your competition, and you have a better idea about who you are, who you married, and the dynamics of your relationship from all sides. It's time to examine the advantages that you have as a wife. There are things you can do to protect your marriage if a poacher is on the prowl, looking to sink her hooks into your husband.

What You're Up Against

Over almost forty years of practice, seeing couples, mate-poachers, singles, and the recently divorced, I've certainly witnessed a broad swath of human behavior. Focusing for now on the predatory other woman (the one most likely to have a personality disorder, as opposed to the accidental or circumstantial affair partner), I can tell you that there's a certain profile that you should be aware of when your radar senses someone honing in on your honey's trail.

When a looter is looking to land a guy—any guy—she knows that she has to put her best foot forward (in Manalos or whatever is featured on the *Maxim* model of the month). She's not only buying the "laddie" mags (*Maxim, Stuff,* and *FHM*)

to keep her finger on male pulse and taste, she could be reading *Penthouse* letters and watching conventional male-pander-
ing porn to perfect her sexual techniques and figure out how to
feed a man's fantasy. That's what she's all about, at least in the
beginning. Even if she wants more from your man than a brief,
easy affair, she'll keep her plan under wraps until he's so deeply
enraptured with her that he'll be unable to let go, for all the
wrong reasons. (To devalue her, you will point that plan out to
your mate.)

In fact, preventing your husband from falling under the
menacing poacher's sexual spell is crucial. You've heard that
the way to a man's heart is through his stomach? Not true.
It's through his mind, by way of his gonads. Another woman
becomes a viable rival to your marriage when your mate feels
invincible or "alive" when he's with her, not you. Although you
know that any love or passion he might feel for this woman
will pass, he probably doesn't. (You will tell him.) What's more,
Helen Fisher, Ph.D., author of *Why We Love: The Nature and
Chemistry of Romantic Love*, reports that men fall in love faster,
harder, and, upon a breakup, suffer much longer—and some
say, deeper—than women. All of these factors add up to profound marital trouble if a trespasser gains access to your partner and is able to sink her teeth into his psyche.

So, what charm does the poacher exude to make a husband gamble his marriage, wife, family, and way of life? Often,
this kind of woman knows instinctively what men want and
what they need. She's familiar with men's emotional and physical needs and weaknesses, and she makes herself available at
just the right time. You already know that a man's genes and
biology make him susceptible to short-term, easy, seemingly
noncommittal sex. If the opportunity happens to arise with a
good-looking woman, his reptilian brain has all the more reason to tell him to go for it—just this once.

In my practice, I've found that whether she's privileged by nature or not, the woman in pursuit makes herself appealing in every way. Every potential mate-poacher I've met in my office knew just how to work it, presenting herself as a special dish to covet and appreciate. She cultivates her appearance by investing in herself to receive maximum returns for the assets she has genetically and socially acquired. Groomed perfectly from her toenails to her tresses, the poacher has a hairstylist, a manicurist, a dermatologist, a personal trainer, and whatever other specialist she might need to make any required adjustments or improvements. The poacher has designed herself to provide your mate pleasure. Appearing fit for his natural selection, she is full of fun and laughs and is receptive to your husband's needs, be they intellectual, emotional, or sexual. She travels light, dresses well, and smells great. Until she's insinuated herself into your man's life, she'll make sure he feels like the king of the world when she's around him. It's all an act on her part, but he'll be in far too deep, far too fast to realize it. You've got to be prepared to take some positive action of your own to keep her away.

The Right "Hot" Stuff

You don't have to look like a model or movie star to be beautiful and alluring. Frankly, while facial attractiveness is important, body shape—that is, normal weight with a small waist-to-hip ratio—seems to be a more potent sex signal than features like a small chin, full lips, and big eyes. (Does anyone think Barbra Streisand has a nice nose? Does anybody care?) No matter what your features look like, getting as healthy and as content as you can will work wonders to maintain that gleam in your own and your husband's eyes. Studies show that you can captivate people by positively interacting with them. For instance, women who smile, make eye contact, and engage the beholder engender better responses than those who don't—even when the women in question have similar physical attributes.

Furthermore, beauty it seems is not only in the eyes of the beholder, it's also in the eyes of the beheld. Consider this Marilyn Monroe factoid. When Marilyn wanted to be left alone in public, all she had to do was tone her dress down and act dowdy. Talking to a friend about how she easily escaped detection in this way, Marilyn decided to show him that she could, just by changing her attitude and carriage, attract immediate attention. She became the "movie star" by simply adjusting her scarf and the way she moved as she walked down the street. Instantly, by a change in attitude, Marilyn transformed herself from ordinary to extraordinary.

The point is that people respond to how you present yourself. When you are in a poacher/wife rivalry, or trying to prevent one, remember to implement the magic of perceived control. Project your sexy, beautiful self out to the world and, of course, to your lawfully wedded husband—or life mate.

Finally, if you (and your guy) believe that beauty is only skin deep, and you are not at all interested in competing with poachers on a superficial level—looking like what you are not, or have no interest in becoming—consider engaging in what some evolutionary experts call "alternate sexual attraction strategies" to retain your mate's marital interest. Focus his attention on the qualities that make you—if not indispensable to your mate—absolutely irreplaceable in his life. Instead of flaunting your long legs or low waist-to-hip ratio, accentuate your solid gold mate traits: cooperation, humor, companionship, devotion, and social/cultural value and alliances.

Embeddedness Benefits

Being a wife gives you the edge in nearly every situation involving your husband and a potential rival. Once you say "I do," an

extensive network of kinsmen and friends—spanning genera-
tions and geography—wraps around your marriage like a protective social web. From a sociological perspective, your martial
bond automatically increases your official kith and kin by a factor of two. Your parents are now your husband's mother- and
father-in-law. His sister is now your sister-in-law, and her son
is now your nephew. Of course, the extent of one's new friends
and relations is perhaps best appreciated when one wins the
mega lottery, but you get the idea. Marriage makes for bigger
clans and formal alliances. (If you doubt this, consider the his-
toric nuptials of European royals over the centuries.)

In fact, once you wed, you are ensconced into the protective layer of both families, whose respective interests are best
served by your productive and reproductively fruitful union.
The more you have, literally and figuratively, the better it is for
both your husband's and your family combined. There's more
children, more money, and more social capital for the clans
that you've united by your vows. The same can be said of your
civic, social, and religious communities that support, collectively, your efforts to raise a family and be righteous, upright
partners and parents. Friends—so long as they are pro-marriage—provide further support for your union. They help when
you need support, care, or comfort.

In large measure, all of the people within this pro-marriage
web will do what they can or must to ensure that your marriage
continues and that your family unit remains intact and safe
from intruders who would do it harm—and they are largely
effective. Research reveals that relationships receiving positive
support from a social network are more stable and less likely to
end. Plus, the more a couple interacts with the network of family, friends, community, and coworkers, the more intense the
support for their union becomes. As you'd expect, the longer
the marriage has lasted, the more deeply others will care if the

relationship continues. Of course, the obverse is also true. A social network can also exert negative influence that works to the detriment of a relationship, destabilizing it and promoting its termination. This is what happens to a poacher when she tells her clan that she's dating your husband and they do what they can to discourage her.

Exploiting Marital Interdependency

Interdependency is a dynamic whereby you and your husband come to rely upon each other for sharing common tasks, holding common memories, and allotting control of your household. Closely related to embeddedness, interdependence intensifies after marriage and grows deeper the longer you are together. Filing joint income-tax returns is a perfect example of interdependency. By signing off on the joint return, you are relying upon each other to be candid and trustworthy, as each of you is jointly and severally liable for whatever tax debts you owe as a unit.

With interdependency based upon trust and time together, you and your mate are able to communicate deeply with minimal words because of your shared context, commitments, and private knowledge. This dynamic of interdependence is a major marital advantage. By its exclusive nature, marital interdependency places a premium on the couple's collective learning and experience, thus emphasizing the "otherness" of anyone else, particularly a potential mate-poacher. By sharing family, friends, a life, and maybe kids, you and your husband become socially, economically, and financially interdependent, apart from how you might feel about each other at any given moment.

What's more, over time, spouses tend to divvy up labor or chores between themselves. Each person develops special skills that amplify and intensify a couple's interdependence. When skills are divided, each spouse depends upon the other for the benefit of the family unit. In this way, interdependence helps to bind a couple through the inevitable ebbs in the tides of love. Ticked off at each other or not, you both continue to rely on each other to execute your agreed upon marital duties and fulfill your respective roles. This is true whether you are the one who gets the groceries and cooks the meals, or makes the money and pays the bills, or cares for the kids and maintains family and social connections (presides over the social calendar, mails the holiday cards, and purchases the gifts for all the proper occasions).

In some instances, both partners contribute their complementary efforts to the marital task at hand, whether it is raising a child, playing tennis, or enjoying sex. In any case, whether a couple shares communal responsibilities or divides them—or does both for the benefit of the relationship—they are promoting marital interdependence, social efficiency, and economic productivity in their household. The relationship between spousal interdependence, economies of scale, and marital satisfaction helped scholars formulate the investment theory of marriage. This theory states that marital commitment is affected by satisfaction in the relationship; attractive, available alternatives; and level of investment in the marriage (as discussed in Chapter 2). Finally, in a functional family, each member helps the other when in need and may have to make some sacrifices until things can be readjusted. The strength ensuing from these generous acts can build the goodwill that can carry you through any tough times you might face.

Giving Good, Um, Attention

Returning to relational satisfaction and wifely advantages, let's examine what so many men say they need to remain content in marriage, connected to their wives, and willing to do anything for her: marital sex. To keep your man's mind on his marriage, and not on his assistant or secretary, it helps to give him what he needs at home.

Being a good spouse means being a good companion. In most cases, that entails a physical as well as an emotional and intellectual communion. In this section, we'll concern ourselves with the sensual and the sexual. Let's begin with a few words about what it means to be a good lover. As the only legal lifetime sexual partner your husband has, you should understand that being a good lover to your husband begins long before you hit the sack. Your value as a sexual companion commences when your clothes are still on. You show him respect, are sensitive to his moods and needs, and honor his trust in you and your marriage. Ultimately, being a good lover is about wanting and learning how to give and receive pleasure.

The Different Drives of Spouses

Though you might be unique, plenty of research proves—and most of my patients confirm—that when sex is involved, men and women sometimes see things very differently. Unlike men, many women require more intimacy before they get in the mood. Some women feel fulfilled more from the emotional aspects of their relationship than its sexual side. Various experts will tell you that a majority of women require coaxing and cuddling before becoming aroused. Unlike men, many women need emotional stimulation to desire sexual activity.

| Don't Sexually or Emotionally Starve Him | "The satiated man and the hungry one do not see the same thing when they look upon a loaf of bread."—Rumi (1207–1273) |

If a man's libido is centered in his penis, you might say a woman's libido revolves around her brain. Simply popping a pill to increase the blood flow to a woman's genitals will not increase her desire if the other important factors are not present. Furthermore, given a woman's biology and the physical costs associated with sex (pregnancy risks and support needed to raise a child), it's no wonder that women require more stimulation to put them in the mood.

Plus, we know that the rewards and costs of sex are different for men and women. In one study, men said that their rewards from sex are feeling comfortable with a partner; feeling good about themselves during or after sex; and having fun during sexual activities. Men cited common costs of sex as these: having it when their partner wasn't in the mood; having a sex life that lacked spontaneity; and enjoying a lower frequency of sexual activities than desired. Women, on the other hand, cited their sexual rewards as being treated well by their partner during sex; being comfortable with their partner; and being with the same partner each time for sex. As for costs, women's top complaints were having sex when not in the mood; a lack of spontaneity in their sex life; and having to spend more time on sex than preferred.

A great way to assess your sexual attitudes and behaviors is to take the Sexual Self-Efficacy Scale for Female Functioning (SSES-F), found in Appendix C. A high score is good; a low score just means that you and your husband have miles to go before you sleep. Have fun. One more thing, when it comes to physical pleasure, ignore the golden rule. Sex is one arena where a good lover doesn't give what she wants; *she gives what her lover wants.* Just because you like it one way doesn't mean your man might not like it another way. I'm not suggesting that you perform any acts you're not comfortable with. I am suggesting that you consider expanding your repertoire to accommodate both your and your husband's tastes and sexual predilections. Remember, you are his only sexual outlet (besides, of course, himself). That's quite a responsibility, but the rewards are also high. Most research confirms that, barring a personality disorder or substance abuse, a sexually satisfied spouse is a happy spouse.

Overcoming Monogamous Monotony

First, humans are one of the 3 percent of mammalian species that are monogamous. So don't fall for the line that people aren't meant to be with just one person. The fact is that people are living twice as long as they once were, and it becomes a challenge to remain with one individual for so long and keep things from getting dull. But before we address ways to maintain that spark of interest in your sex life, let's pause to review the benefits of sticking with your spouse, and vice versa, over the years.

Married people consistently rate themselves as happier and more sexually active than their single counterparts. Why? Spouses are available to each other, and they are safe. Marriage is the one U.S. social institution where sex between two adults is actually encouraged. Many people find this social approval very freeing. Witness the Christian-Sex.net Web site, which promises "A guaranteed step-by-step game plan to experience deeper and more intense sexual pleasure and fulfillment . . . excitement . . . and sexual interest from your wife!" Even the devout want in on the married fun.

Furthermore, married people have invested serious time and effort into learning what pleases their spouse, as opposed to spending time on other matters. Once you know what pleasures your mate enjoys, there's no learning curve to suffer through once you hit the sack. Your husband knows what you like and where you like it. (If not, you must have a talk and complete the SSES Scale in Appendix C.) Consequently, what little you lose in newness you gain in being a sure bet, a safe harbor, and a repository of your husband's sexual predilections. If not, it's something to strive for.

Of course, being a kind, dependable lover doesn't mean that you must close yourself off from the possibility of the novel and the exciting. Variety and spontaneity can spice things up for a married couple. Why not do with your spouse what you'd try with a new person? I've learned from my practice that the typical mate-poacher is usually up to speed on the latest sexual trends. One of my patients (a would-be poacher on the prowl) was using Altoids to do more than freshen her breath the moment she learned that Ms. Monica Lewinsky wanted to employ them in the White House in ways that the maker doesn't advertise. Remember, the woman who wants to sexually ensnare your husband works out on every level: her body, her flirting, and her sexual techniques. The mate-poacher has learned to please, attract, and captivate a man in the short term. She knows that a good romp in the hay can keep your guy interested in her for at least a few hours, and, if she plays her cards right, perhaps a few days, which can lead to weeks, which can lead to real trouble. This is what you are up against. (Wife hint: I'm told that the instantly dissolving, Cool Mint Listerine PocketPaks are the Altoids of the new millennium.)

Though a purely sexual relationship does not generally have the stuff that makes for a lasting, committed relationship, it's

This Is No English Wallpaper Designer

If you see a bill that says Ashley Madison, beware. It's a dating site for marrieds whose motto is "When monogamy becomes monotony." Check it out for yourself online at *www .ashleymadison.com*.

often enough to place a serious, if not fatal, strain on a marriage, and the mate-poacher knows this. Fact is, she's counting on it. As the wife, your best defense against this kind of encounter—beginning as a purely sexual adventure—is to meet your husband's needs at home. Do you have to go crazy every night? No, that would become boring and too much work. Make your sex life fun and spontaneous for both of you, and don't feel pressured to do anything that feels wrong or uncomfortable for either of you. Find your mutual area of interest and comfort.

One of my patients takes her husband out to the backyard pool as soon as summer arrives and they skinny dip in it with great regularity. Her husband is a very happy man due to his wife's nude aquatics. Another of my patients commandeers the family digital camcorder, and using a private chip, records X-rated fun and frolic with her husband. When they are finished "shooting," they pop out their adult-only chip, lock it away, and reinsert the family-safe chip so no one's the wiser. She gives her husband the private chip when he has to go away on business trips. When he's in his hotel room, he views her doing something wonderful to him and they engage in mutually satisfying, mate-retaining, masturbatory phone sex. Use your imagination and do whatever works for you. By maintaining arousal, fantasy, and novelty you have the power to make your marital love bond far more satisfying than anything the poacher could offer your husband.

CHAPTER 8

The Marital Emergency

This chapter examines what happens when the unthinkable turns out to be factual. In other words, despite your efforts and/or your complete ignorance, the first four stages of extramarital involvement (predisposition, approach, initial involvement, and perhaps, maintenance) have occurred. Now, you are dealing with the last two stages of infidelity: disclosure (or discovery) and response. But before we begin addressing your options for action after discovering that your husband had—or is having—an affair (whether emotional and/or sexual), let's outline the topic. Identifying the problem, after all, is the first step toward its resolution.

Undressing Infidelity

Scores of experts—therapists, counselors, psychoanalysts, physicians, scholars, and researchers—disagree on the official definition of "infidelity." For a spouse whose husband has betrayed her, semantics pose little problem. When it comes to infidelity, she knows it when she sees it—or suspects it or senses it. Still, it's important to understand what professionals mean when they refer to the topic. There are those who believe that infidelity occurs when a couple's "dyadic norms" are violated. This is jargon for a couple's boundaries, which separate the things that belong strictly in the domain of their private unit from what's allowed between the two in the outside world. The couple decides on the limits of closeness—physical and emotional—allowed between a spouse and a third party.

When I think about the concept of couple boundaries, I recall a Leonard Cohen radio interview from the early 1990s. Cohen was describing a married couple; the wife, Suzanne, was the namesake for his famously beautiful song. Mr. Cohen said of Suzanne and her husband, "as a couple they were inviolate, you just didn't intrude into that kind of shared glory that they manifested." Because Mr. Cohen knew he didn't have a chance of successfully seducing the happily married Suzanne, he mused about touching her perfect body with his mind, the closest he knew he'd ever get.

When a couple doesn't send out the vibe that they are gloriously inviolate, or if one of them invites an outsider into a formerly private aspect of their life, betrayal has occurred and infidelity is committed against the other half of the couple. Usually, this third party is the opposite sex of the involved spouse, though not always. An example of emotional infidelity could be a relationship between your husband and a colleague (male or female) in whom he confides private thoughts and feelings and from whom he takes advice about personal matters, leaving you, his spouse, out of *their* private, intimate loop.

Other researchers define infidelity as requiring an element of sexual contact, though not necessarily including intercourse. This is unlike President Clinton's infamous testimony during his 1998 deposition, when he said his response depended upon what the meaning of "is" is. No matter how you define it or want to parse words, if a husband has sexual contact with someone other than his wife, without her consent, then he's crossed the line from faithfulness to infidelity. While taking intercourse off the table—so to speak—can eliminate the risk of the third party's pregnancy, and in some cases may reduce the chances of acquiring an STD, behavior involving the private parts of either a spouse or a third party—or both—is verboten, and certainly beyond what most would tolerate from a spouse. There are many different ways to describe and interpret infidelity or extramarital involvement. We'll assume for our purposes that having an affair means having violated a spouse's trust and honor by breaching the rules that the couple set up for themselves.

Finally, a limiting word here might be helpful. In the view of most professionals, a spouse's thoughts don't count as infidelity, so long as the couple is comfortable with how each partner processes his or her feelings. Even masturbation after marriage is common and healthy. Most professionals would not put that behavior in the category of infidelity, unless the couple defined the behavior as a breach of trust or intimacy between them. Similarly, nonaddictive, occasional enjoyment of sexually explicit media or having sexual thoughts or fantasies about others is perfectly normal, healthy behavior, particularly for men. If both spouses handle the fantasies appropriately, they can provide an excellent source of adult fun, keeping your love life and sexual connection vital and active. (One night you play the French maid, the next night he plays the airline captain—some role-playing is fine.) It really all boils down to what you and your husband agree is acceptable and what is not. You and your mate can decide if the original rules are still right for you, or whether a rethinking is in order.

Understanding the Damage

The first step in dealing with extramarital involvement (also referred to here as infidelity, affair, and extramarital sex) is defining it. With that done, it's time now to focus on the feelings you are likely to experience upon discovery of an affair and how to handle yourself when the traumatic news hits home that your husband has betrayed, dishonored, and deceived you.

You probably don't need a shrink to tell you that you'll be upset and probably surprised (unless you had a conscious or unconscious role in promoting the affair, and thus received secondary benefits that we'll discuss later). There are other classic symptoms you might never suspect, but that will surface, nonetheless, once you process your husband's betrayal and what it means to your relationship, your family, your life, your view of your spouse, and most important, your perception of yourself.

Though you expect to experience anger, another reaction that is almost as common, but far less anticipated, is depression. You might have done everything right as a wife; perhaps your husband's personality disorder, lack of character or maturity, or substance-abuse problem was the root of his unfaithful behavior. Yet you are still likely to turn your anger inward and suffer despair and severe anxiety in the first few months after you learn about the affair. In fact, depression and suicidal thoughts are common reasons that a woman will enter therapy after learning of her mate's infidelity.

Likewise, upon learning of an affair, some women respond as if they've been wounded in battle, suffering shell shock or post-traumatic stress disorder symptoms (flashbacks, startle responses, repeating nightmares, insomnia, and disassociation or numbing) similar to that which some combatants suffer after war. From this woman's psychological perspective, the battle was brought into the most intimate area of her life and she's been gravely injured by it.

If the affair has completely taken you by surprise, you are most at risk for severe symptoms. You might find yourself obsessing over the details of his affair, for instance, revisiting in your mind where your husband must have been when he told you he was somewhere else. Your mind may dwell on who she was and how you compare to her. Wives frequently insist that their husbands reveal every iota of fact about their transgressions. This stance is often not helpful, and a therapist can guide you through the maze of what factors heal and which do more harm where affair details are concerned. Other wives insist that their husbands leave the home or move out of the marital bedroom until they can come to an understanding of how and why the betrayal occurred. Other reactions include insisting on husbands calling in every few hours or being available at any time the wife chooses to make contact. Hypervigilance and suspicion are natural consequences after betrayal, and these responses vary from woman to woman.

Even if you decide to make a go of your marriage, the discovery or disclosure of an affair typically induces profound feelings of loss and sadness. What was once is no more, as your circle of two has been breached. You'll enter into a mourning phase, but without the automatic social support bestowed upon a person who suffers other severe losses such as a death, illness, or accidental physical injury befalling a loved one.

For some wives, misplaced feelings of shame, embarrassment, or guilt keep them from reaching out for support through this difficult time, leaving them isolated when they most need help from friends or trained professionals. No matter who you see for help or how you cope, be on notice for Elisabeth Kübler-Ross's five phases (denial, anger, bargaining, depression, and acceptance) that are sure to arise after receiving the initially catastrophic news of your husband's betrayal and the losses it portends. According to Kübler-Ross's theory, your grief will be as genuine as the faith you once had in your husband and your marriage.

Overall, you can expect to face an emotional roller coaster within the first few months, followed by a cease fire during which you'll regroup (known to experts as the "moratorium" phase), and, finally, a period during which you will try to make sense of what happened in your marriage and why. If you choose to remain married, you will begin the trust-building process; if not, you'll try to resolve the infidelity, learning from it so you can move on to the next phase of your life improved by the experience, wiser, and more watchful.

Finally, the way a woman learns of the affair normally makes a difference in how she reacts and copes to the news. Studies show that women who learn about their husbands' affairs directly, from the husband, have a better chance of recovering quicker. Chances for saving the marriage are greater than when she hears the news from a third party (friend or foe) or discovers the affair herself. One of the most painful scenarios for a wife is dealing with a husband who has repeatedly lied to her, denying her suspicions, and who is then revealed to have been having an affair all along. In this case, a woman must contend with her spouse's utter disregard of the truth and respect for her and her marriage. Recovery under circumstances threaded with treachery through and through is long and difficult, if possible at all.

Confronting Your Husband

No matter how angry you are, or what you know—or think you know—or how you received the information about the affair, I urge you to use good sense and reason in all things and actions. Consider the cautionary tale of the beautiful, successful, law-abiding Houston dentist, Clara Harris. Dr. Harris, you might recall, was the wife who killed her fellow dentist husband in a Texas hotel parking lot, running him over several times with her Mercedes, after finding him with the mistress he was supposed to have left behind. In five short minutes, Dr. Harris's entire life changed from wronged, wealthy wife and mother to murderer, all because she completely lost her impulse control when her husband chose his mistress over her.

Under those volatile circumstances, when a person feels so enraged and so violated, it's much easier to act irrationally— still knowing what's right and what's wrong, mind you, but for the moment, simply not caring. How do you protect yourself from getting into irreparable trouble and criminal prosecution? Avoid engaging in any *in flagrante delicto* (Latin for "while the crime still burns") confrontations, ever. Aristotle aptly noted, *"Anyone can become angry—that is easy. But to be angry at the right person, to the right degree, at the right time, for the right purpose, and in the right way—that is not easy."* Don't be tempted to put yourself and your spouse in a perilous situation. While you think you might be able to handle what you may find, you might not. After all, you are only human. You know your anger will pass, but murder and mayhem are permanent.

Avoid violence and disaster by moving forward to face your husband with dignity and discipline. When you have regained your composure and feel ready for a talk, pick a psychologically safe and physically secure place for the two of you to meet and discuss the matter at hand. When you arrive, you will be ready, poised, and able to articulate your feelings and whatever wishes you have for yourself, your family, and your future.

Preparing for the Husband Talk

You know that communication can be easily misconstrued, not only along verbal lines (words, tone, and even the tempo of speech), but also through nonverbal gestures, postures, and positions. After you've collected yourself, the first thing you want to do is figure out what you want to accomplish by having this conversation with your husband. If you want to confront your spouse simply to scream or rant, skip it. Instead, go to your therapist, support group, or good friend. This has a better chance of putting you in a good place, one where you stand to gain more from your husband than his retroactive justification that he had the right to cheat on such a shrew.

Plan for a moderate encounter. Rehearsing in your mind what you will say and imagining how you will respond emotionally should your mate be hostile or uncommunicative will serve you well. Some people find it helpful to construct the entire dialogue in their minds or on paper to prepare them for the occasion. In most endeavors, preparation reduces anxiety, and in this case, anything that reduces apprehension is good. Plus, thinking ahead of time about what to say and how to say it provides you with a means to remain calm and keep your emotions in check. Because you've thought the issues through beforehand, you can make superior arguments and offer better replies than if you had not prepared at all.

Explain What You've Learned

I've suggested what you shouldn't say (as in, ranting is generally not productive), but here I have a positive recommendation. Presenting yourself as the wounded but graceful wife is usually a winning combination, as your husband's guilt and regret can cause him to do almost anything you request, particularly if he's admitted his mistake and wishes to atone and work for forgiveness. Moreover, if you want him back, or think you do—or at least don't want "her" to get him—consider teaching your husband everything you've learned about love and his temporary attraction to the other woman. While you're not excusing his behavior you are giving him a scientific hook upon which to hang his remorseful hat, should you welcome him back home.

The Coolidge Effect and the Dopamine High

We know that dopamine is the driving force for much of human behavior as it controls the reward center of the brain.

Moreover, other "rush" stimulating chemicals, such as dopamine, adrenaline, phenylethylamine (aka PEA—found in chocolate), and beta-endorphins (endogenous opioids—think ready-made, legal morphine or heroin) soar when one is in the midst of new love. Serotonin drops and we become nearly compulsive in our mental desires to ruminate about, concentrate on, and just be with the object of our enormous physical craving. There's another factor that could influence your husband's unfaithful behavior. Though not proven to exist in primates, we know the phenomenon exists on the farm and in much of the animal kingdom; it's worth a mention as it appears in some of the academic literature on sex and biology. Called the Coolidge effect, it refers to the fact that a male mammal (think goat, horse, rat—okay, maybe husband) will initially mate many times with a female, after which he will lose all sexual interest in her. Even if her face is covered (no, this is not

The Chicken and the President

Though we'll never know for sure which came first, the term "Coolidge effect" derives from a charming story about President Calvin Coolidge, his wife, Grace, and their visit to a Kentucky chicken farm. Given separate tours upon their arrival, rumor has it that Grace asked her escort how often the rooster performed his duties. His response was "Dozens of times each day." Grace's reply: "Please, tell that to the president." When the escort did as requested, the president paused and then asked him whether the rooster was with the same chicken. The response was no, it was a different chicken each time. The president replied: "Please, tell *that* to Mrs. Coolidge."

getting personal, just giving the facts here) and her vaginal scent is masked, the shrewd male mammal is not misled and will not mate with the female he's already had, even if no other choice is provided to him. For him, the good times are over and he will simply not have sex.

But put another filly in his paddock and it's a different story. He'll become a regular stud, so to speak, mating multiple times with the new female. Soon, however, he'll tire of her, sexually (though he'll still want her to make his oats and keep the barn tidy). When the next filly comes along, once again, this male mammal is ready to perform. Good-bye celibacy, hello satyriasis. And so it goes, on and on.

Again, no one can say with any reasonable degree of scientific certainty that the Coolidge effect is found in men. It certainly would not give them license to cheat or be promiscuous, yet it's interesting and gives one pause. In the meantime, when you meet your mate to discuss your relationship, offer him information about sexual behavior in general and natural amphetamines (dopamine and adrenaline), serotonin, and PEA, in particular. Explain that the feelings (empathy, euphoria, disinhibition, increased sensuality, and so on) he has now for his lover (if he has any) are merely chemical and chimerical and will not last. Furthermore, you can offer him the statistics about unsuccessful relationships between men and their mistresses, as more than 60 percent of those marriages fail—and how you're willing to work with him if he promises to apologize and understand the harm and hurt he's caused, for no good reason.

On the downside, if he's still smack in the middle of passion, be prepared for him to act like a lovesick puppy that is not yet ready to give up his new play pal. Remember, if the affair is recent or ongoing, his brain has been assaulted with high dopamine, making him like a junkie in need of a fix. I'm not excusing his behavior but simply explaining what could be going on in his biochemistry. Plus, he might be obsessing over the affair due to his lowered serotonin while his elevated PEA impairs his judgment, thoughts, and perceptions. All this is making his lover seem all the good that you know (and will tell him) she is not. Moreover, if your husband is the anxious type, he might be especially vulnerable to falling in love as he might have a faulty serotonin transporter gene that makes him feel fear and exhilaration more than the average guy and that is also now making him feel that he's in love more than the norm. Fear and feeling in love have been linked by researchers for years now. In fact, the secrecy of an affair might be enough to fool a man into thinking it's love, when it's really only the buzz of doing something surreptitious and illicit that stimulates the brain into feeling the thrill of new romance.

Keeping Mature Love Alive

Thirty-some years ago, researchers performed what has come to be known as the bridge study. The women whom men met while walking over a precarious suspension bridge seemed more attractive than the women the men met while on a safe foot bridge—even though the women from both bridges were equally attractive. These findings suggest that circumstances inducing physiological arousal made a person's companion seem more attractive. Some scientists suggest doing something new together or taking up a risky sport like skiing or skydiving—anything that will crank up that feeling of excitement, causing fear and physiological cues of arousal that both of you can mutually confuse as fresh passion and renewed attraction.

All the same, don't despair. Biology might be mysterious, but it's not malicious. Vasopressin and oxytocin are the loving attachment hormones that work to cement the emotional bond between a man and a woman long after the romance ends. Research tells us that loving and nurturing behaviors on your part, such as soothing strokes and affectionate caresses, can reignite the release of oxytocin in his brain, where it works its magic on the limbic system. Not only can the oxytocin release make him warmly disposed toward you, it reduces his craving for high dopamine levels associated with new love or illicit sex. Oxytocin can also promote healing, reduce stress (lowering cortisol), and increase a man's potency. Finally, unlike dopamine, a hormone with down-regulating receptors (the more that's released, the more you want, but the more you have to do to get it), oxytocin flows freely. Your body produces the same amounts each time you engage in the same level of activity.

While intimate, nurturing companionship and loving touch can stimulate the release of oxytocin, to get the vasopressin flowing, you might have to break down and share an orgasm with your husband. The power of good old loving mutual sex can never be underestimated. Still, given the fact of your mate's infidelity, you understandably might not be in the mood (or his blood work might not have come back yet). Do as little or as much as you want. It's up to you.

Dealing Directly with HER

What happens if the mate-poacher confronts you? This is not the norm. Once the other woman shoots her load, she loses her power, which stems from maintaining secrecy of the affair. If she uses her leverage and makes contact with you, she loses it with your husband. That's it. Game's over, cat's out of the bag (and any other cliché you'd care to insert). Still, if the other woman does choose to contact you, as the wife you must maintain the power and dignity your status confers upon you. In contrast, as an interloper and intruder into the marriage, the other woman does not deserve your time or respect. If there's a discussion to be had, it should be at your command and convenience, on turf and terms of your choosing. If, however, you are caught by the other woman and are unable to escape her prepared encounter (say in an elevator or a public place, or the Little Nell in Aspen a la Marla and Ivana Trump, circa 1989), I urge you to regally dismiss her as the nonentity she is, to you anyhow.

As for your seeking the mistress out, fine, but if you insist on speaking, be ready for an earful whether you communicate by phone, fax, computer, or in person. To engage the mate-poacher in conversation is usually to ask for trouble. But if that's what you must do, make sure to maintain your decorum and remain calm and be prepared for her to prove to you just how intimate she's become with your husband (true or not). Telling you that she was the one to purchase your son's graduation gift or that she and your husband are planning a life together is to be expected. Remember, the other woman is not dating your husband to be kind to you. Besides, Shakespeare had it right: "O beware, my lord, of jealousy; It is the green eyed monster which doth mock the meat it feeds on." In this case, she is probably more jealous of you than you would ever be of her: You hold all the cards, she gets your crumbs. So don't expect anything good to come from your chat. Consider yourself warned, and proceed with caution and dignity.

Evaluating EMI

Whether he's completely checked out of your marriage or broken your vows once during a drunken one-night stand can make a difference as to what you do next. You might want to know whether the third party is ready and waiting to replace you or if she wanted your man for an evening of fun, nothing more, and no matter the costs to him or certainly to you. In order to find out what you're up against, let's review what we know about affairs themselves. In this way, you'll gain more insight into who your mate is, why he strayed, and the type of woman involved. It's important to know whether she'll be a factor in your life or a bump in the road that you can put behind you, after you've traveled the long distance from shock, recovery, and forgiveness, to marital renewal—or not. Hopefully, once you ascertain the kind of infidelity that's occurred and the type of affair that resulted, you'll be able to better judge what your options are and how to go about implementing your plan, depending upon what you feel is best for you, your marriage, and perhaps your kids.

There have been many books and articles written about extramarital involvement. Though many are not scientifically tested, some of these theories can help you by providing a framework to analyze your own situation. Let's have a look at some of the popular notions of the kinds of affairs people have, and the acts they are premised on. In the mid 1990s, professionals Frank S. Pittman and Tina Pittman Wagers wrote that most extramarital involvement falls into four basic categories:

Accidental: The affair is unplanned and, though wrong, is really a result of circumstance (such as a one-night stand during a business trip).

Habitual: In this scenario, the husband is a Don Juan who needs to score, the more the better. It doesn't matter how wonderful his wife is or how great this philanderer has it at home.

Passionate: This kind of affair poses the most critical threat to a marriage because it involves romantic love, where the husband feels all the things for the lover that he's supposed to feel for a wife. He's likely to believe that his lover is a true soul mate and might have a difficult time quitting her, as it were.

Condoned infidelity: This arrangement arises in connection with a wife's permission, and so this affair is a sanctioned part of the martial pact.

As far as you're concerned, except for the last category, all extramarital involvement is unacceptable, but some forms are more damaging than others.

Accidental
The one-night stand is generally ill-advised and often profoundly regretted when the husband realizes the harm he's done to his marriage and the pain he's caused his wife for not much comparative pleasure. Unless the one-night stand results in a pregnancy or an STD, the couple can often move on, so long as the wife is willing to forgive and the husband is willing to accept responsibility for what he's done and seek atonement and works on trust-building again.

Habitual
The habitual cheater will not change unless he undergoes serious analysis or therapy to gain insight into his behavior. This requires him to gain an understanding about his cultural or social identity in terms of how it promotes this behavior. It might also mean understanding the personality disorder (usually narcissistic, borderline, or antisocial) from which he suffers or addressing any substance abuse problems that compound the problem. If you are married to this kind of man, you either have to live with the likelihood that his womanizing will continue, and decide that all things considered, it's worth it to you

to remain married, or you have to get out. It is usually your choice as this kind of man is not looking for a new wife, just a new thrill.

Passionate

The passionate affair is the wife's worst nightmare because it generally means that the husband has fallen in love—hard, fast, and helplessly. This is the exact situation where telling him about brain chemistry might do you some good. Your goal is to make him understand that the euphoria he's now feeling will dissipate over time (two to four years per our knowledge of biochemistry), and then he'll be right back to where he was with you—loving, but not living in the throes of hot, passionate, lusty love.

Condoned

For many couples, sex is not important to one or both. If both, they can have a companionate marriage, without sex. If only one spouse feels this way, then you're likely to have a look-the-other-way arrangement in which the "sexual" spouse can indulge his physical desires, so long as all parties are discreet and respectful of each other. Physical gratification is the single goal of these affairs, not marriage-threatening love, attachment, or social connection. Additionally, there are marriages ("open" or "swinging") where the partners are sexual with each other but also agree that one or both of them are allowed to have sex with others. The affair partners are not meant to interfere with the marriage relationship; rather, they serve to add spice and variety to the couple's sexual life. Aside from human jealousy, these affairs can threaten even an "open" marriage when one of the sexual partners (third party or spouse) falls in love—unexpectedly or not—and wants more of the lover and less of the spouse.

Affair Typology, Part Two

In the early 1990s, a social worker named Emily Brown wrote about affairs from a slightly different point of view. Her extramarital involvement categories are arranged according to the purpose the marital purpose served:

Conflict avoiding: These mates lack communication and conflict-resolution skills, so instead of dealing with their relationship issues, they find others to connect with.

Intimacy avoiding: These mates use affairs as a way to avoid getting too close to each other. In addition to the affair, they might use conflict as a means of erecting a wall between themselves and their spouses.

Pain numbing: These partners engage in extramarital involvement as a result of sexual addiction, as they are compelled to have sex with others to numb psychic pain associated with other issues like childhood abuse or a personality disorder, particularly borderline.

Filling unmet or neglected needs: In a "split-self affair," a spouse tries to maintain his marriage in spite of neglected and unmet needs and finds a lover who will fulfill them ("his other side"). This lover is a pseudospouse, and the affair is often long-term, nurturing, and loving. This type of affair can break a marriage, as the other woman can be considered a serious, spouse-like rival.

Justifying the end: In an "exit affair," the partner has already decided he's out of the marriage, but instead of discussing it with his spouse, he has an affair to end the relationship with his wife.

Unless sanctioned, you will be in pain upon learning of any affair. And while some spouses will cheat no matter what due to personality disorders, chemical abuse, or a cultural sense of entitlement (the proverbial "machismo"), most affairs reveal a problem within the marriage relationship. This is hopeful news because it means that you and your spouse can do something to fix whatever was broken or not functioning well in your relationship, which allowed a lapse that ultimately resulted in an affair.

But before you can learn what went wrong, or how to make it right, most couples require professional help for guidance, feedback, and more.

Therapeutic Intervention

Most couples facing the trauma of infidelity (or even those who are experiencing relational difficulties, preinfidelity) will benefit from the good offices of a well-trained, ethical couple therapist (or marriage counselor). At a time when the marriage is in crisis, the betrayed spouse is traumatized, and the involved spouse is in deep relational difficulty. Couple therapy offers a

A Therapeutic Caution

Thinking of an affair as the result of a disease model and using a twelve-step program can be helpful and effective in many cases involving substance abuse, use, or dependency. But be cautious about declaring someone a sex addict without a professional diagnosis. If that's not the real issue, it will not help and could destroy any chance you have of truly understanding what is going on in your spouse's head and why he is acting, feeling, and perceiving as he is.

means for a troubled pair to gain an unbiased clinical assessment of problems (such as whether mental illness, a personality disorder, or chemical dependency is present in either spouse); appropriate intervention to improve functioning; and feedback on how the couple is doing as they learn new ways to deal with or modify old habits and patterns.

Although infidelity is not the only reason couples seek counseling, it is a common problem that therapists see every day. Moreover, therapists rank infidelity as the second most damaging issue a relationship can endure. (Physical abuse ranks number one.) You can be assured that what you are feeling and thinking is notoriously difficult but also that it can be addressed effectively with professional assistance.

Why not go it alone? Because it is nearly impossible to diagnose and fix problems that you can't see for all the reasons you didn't see them when they were happening. In most instances, with the help of an effective couple therapist, you'll learn how and why, as a couple, unhealthy forces were able to penetrate the walls of your marriage, and how you can, with help, persistence, and mutual good faith, seal those cracks and mend those fences between you.

Types of Therapy

Though generally lumped together under the catchall term "couple therapy" or marital counseling, different approaches are favored by different therapists. Here are a few of the most popular theories to consider:

EFT (emotional-focused therapy): EFT is one of the most widely used marital therapies, second only to behavioral approaches. Emotions and affect (emotionally focused interventions) are used to change the couples' response to each other. This therapy recognizes the role of early attachment problems in relationships and helps couples change destructive patterns into trusting ones. The goal of the therapist is to promote emotional bonding between the couple that will alter their relationship in positive ways.

Object relations: This theory sees people as social animals with the need for love objects. The therapist works with defenses against anxiety that promote unhealthy behaviors. The therapist plays an important role in motivating change and uses transference and counter-transference to give the couple insight to their behavior. The goal is to promote caring and respect for self, and then as a couple, and for each other.

Bowen's family systems theory: Dr. Murray Bowen developed this theory of human behavior based on family systems. Bowen's theory helps a couple develop insight into their family of origin systems with direction on invoking behavioral change. The final goal of this therapy is to allow couples or families to have more honest and effective ways of relating to each other and their families and to be self differentiated.

The contextual approach: Originated by Ivan Boszormenyi-Nagy, this theory involves the couple's characteristics, their interpersonal relationships, personalities, needs, past relationships, family systems, occupations, stressors, and other life influences. This theory focuses on the treatment of couples as individuals and considers family needs, exploring positive and negative behaviors. The goal is to improve relationship problems through modifying behavior and establishing the self in both partners.

Cognitive behavioral therapy (CBT): This is the combination of two kinds of psychotherapy. Cognitive therapy deals with the thought processes that might underlie a person's maladaptive behaviors, and behavioral therapy deals with the conduct that occurs on account of the thoughts (anger, fear, depression, and so on). In traditional psychotherapy, a patient looks for insight into his behavior and thoughts, whereas in CBT, the therapist helps the couple to change behaviors by showing them erroneous or faulty thought processes. A CB therapist takes an active role in helping a couple explore cognitive and behavioral processes. The goal is to learn new ways of thinking and behaviors (including communication skills and problem-solving) to resolve conflict in the marriage. Finally, CBT is much quicker (often no more than twenty sessions) than traditional therapy, which can take years.

Insight-oriented marital therapy: This therapy helps the patient understand and explore his behavior. The goal is to explore unconscious or underlying thoughts or behaviors, uncover the unconscious conflicts, and bring them under conscious awareness. Once that occurs, the therapist helps the patient change his dysfunctional behaviors.

Gestalt: This theory is named for the German word meaning shape or form. Gestalt theory addresses the here and now, promoting awareness of the patient's own feelings and behaviors. The goal of this therapy is to have the patient self-heal by understanding his behaviors.

Eclectic: A term used by a therapist who will treats patients using the most appropriate forms of therapy from the various modalities available.

Whatever type of marital therapy you select, the most important feature of couple counseling is for each of you to believe that your therapist is bright, fair, unbiased between you, and, most important, up to the challenge of helping you understand and fix what led your husband to succumb to the mate-poacher in the first place.

No matter the type of therapy or therapist you choose, when you enter an office for couple therapy, the first item on the agenda is usually to identify the purpose of the therapy. Are you there to deal with the infidelity and rebuild the marriage; deal with the infidelity and your ambivalence about continuing the relationship; or to make sense of what happened, then dissolve the marriage? (Most therapists would not want you to make such a life-altering decision upon the first few weeks after discovering the affair. Like any other trauma, you'll need time before you can make rationally sound judgments about a major life event.) If you want to remain married, but your spouse wants out (or vice versa), the therapist will suggest an effective way of dealing with both of your desires, bearing in mind what is therapeutic versus what would be harmful to each of you at any given time. Whatever you and your spouse decide will determine how the sessions are handled.

After you and your spouse articulate your objectives in therapy, you'll be ready to work on your issues. In the beginning, the therapist will do what is necessary to maintain a space in which a couple can discuss difficult issues while working toward constructive resolution. Taking a therapeutic role, the counselor can help a couple address poisonous emotions and point out and help change destructive behavior patterns (such as controlling, overfunctioning, threatening, defensive, counter-attacking, or withdrawing actions) that triggered problems in the marriage before the affair.

Once you have established a rapport with the counselor, she or he will help you and your partner address issues like power struggles, boundary problems, and roles established during your marriage, examining each topic for how it worked for or against you and your goals for your relationship and why. If you have children, the therapist will consider how they fit into your family system, as well as any other people who influence your life as a married unit.

Though painful in the beginning, marital therapy can ease a couple through that painful roller-coaster phase that most face upon disclosure of a spouse's infidelity. By the end of the process, many spouses feel they have gained insights into how their communication and conflict-resolution skills and ways of thinking, feeling (fears of abandonment, control, or intimacy), acting, and perceiving (not understanding each one's hot button issues) contributed to the marital problems that eventually manifested themselves in the infidelity. With work and help, a couple can restructure how they act and react alone and with each other, allowing each spouse a way of growing and developing into a more functional, content partner and human.

How Couple and Individual Therapy Differ

There is a difference between couple or marital counseling—often sought in the short run in times of crisis—and longer-term individual therapy, in which a person addresses the deeper problems that gave rise to the marital issues that caused an affair—or a very close call.

Almost invariably, with couple therapy, the people are more resistant to change. They are there on account of a crisis, like infidelity, or another distinct problem like anger management, addiction, overspending, communication conflicts, or general marital dissatisfaction. On the other hand, when a person seeks individual therapy, she's usually there of her own accord, seeking help for herself, not someone else. She is not seeking change for another person's benefit; she's seeking insight, change for her own benefit. Individual therapy is explored more in later chapters.

CHAPTER 9

Exploiting Your Spousal Prerogatives

Remember the saying, ownership is nine tenths of the law? Well, it's partially true, metaphorically speaking. You've got the home, the family, the shared history with your husband, and a deeper knowledge of his psyche—not to mention the full weight of legal support and moral authority.

Gathering Your Allies

Nothing is new under the sun. From the beginning of time, otherwise sensible, reasonable, honorable humans have left their homes, abandoning mates and children, all because they've "fallen" in love or found passion with someone new. Unlike times before, however, today's science informs us that infatuation, with all its physical manifestations, is temporary by biochemical design and rarely worth the cost of leaving the life and lover that you already have. Sometimes hearing these facts from someone other than a spouse (such as a sibling, friend, parent, or uncle) is enough to make a husband stop and think about what he's about to do—especially if there's a business or reputation at stake and a public divorce would cause all sorts of legal woes for everyone involved.

We've already discussed how as social animals people depend upon their fellow humans for survival. (Recall, no man is an island.) Living among a network of loved ones and kin provides a person with a sense of belonging and peace, as well as mutual allegiance and support. (We are a tribal species, after all.) The family will protect its general interests as it promotes the individual well-being of its affiliates. When your marriage is threatened, your network can help you, depending upon your relationship with its members and the dynamics of the families within the group. Some family members will respond to a call for help by offering to run interference. In-laws, for instance, might take their kin (your husband) aside and try to find out what's happening and set the matter right in a way that accommodates all affected. Not everyone will take an active role, however. Some family members will refuse to get involved; others won't see a problem, especially if infidelity was the norm in their household. (If they put up with it, you can too.) But for the most part, families do not encourage infidelity and will be there for you as a form of unified support, particularly if you have children.

Naturally, before family members can come to your aid, they must know of the imminent danger. Though many people find it difficult to discuss marital trouble—especially if a third party is involved—it is a necessary antecedent for rounding the troops to your defense. Consider confiding in one trusted family member so he or she can offer you emotional (and maybe financial) support. This confidant could perhaps use his or her personal influence over your husband, and others in his circle as well, to explain the damage that could be irreparably wreaked upon your family if he leaves you for a stranger or continues fooling around, risking your permanent departure.

As a generally competent person, think about how you can best use your social support network in a time of need. Your wifely status not only gives you the benefit of a loyal family—definitely yours, and often his—it also offers the advantage of having the entire community (religious leaders, mutual friends, neighbors, and colleagues who support you and your marriage) show open and notorious support for your position. There's no question concerning the villain's identity in your drama. From a community point of view, the woman having an affair with *your husband* is an evil doer and home-wrecker and should be brusquely dismissed. (She is a threat to everyone's marriage as she flouts decorum and disrespects boundaries and legal and moral obligations.)

But to set the wheels in motion you must disclose your need for help. Bear in mind, humans who remain isolated do not generally fair as well as those who can rely upon others to help them. If you can't work your problems out with your spouse or your therapist, show yourself to be one of Darwin's adapters and seek support, if you need it. Even if you ultimately decide that staying together is not feasible, giving yourself the benefit of social support at a critical time of need can provide you with comfort and the moral high ground no matter what comes to pass as a consequence of others' ignoble actions.

Home-Wreckers Not Welcome

Widespread community and family backing for you and your marriage are found on one end of the relationship support scale; universal opprobrium for a secret affair with a married partner is found on the other. Unless your husband is brazen or itching for a marital exit (for all those reasons addressed in earlier chapters), if he's engaging in an extramarital affair, chances are very good that he's tried to keep it a secret. Even if you've recently learned about the transgression, it's likely that the interloper has not shared information about her affair with friends and family. Think about it. Who in their right mind would brag about being involved with a man whose primary and legal relationship is to another woman and her kin?

Even at this secular time in history, most people in civil society do not condone home-wrecking or esteem acts of betrayal, disloyalty, or deceit—apart from the world of entertainment, where mate-stealing seems sanctioned as part of the show under the big tent. (Angelina Jolie, Marla Maples, Michelle Phillips, Yoko Ono, Elizabeth Taylor, and Suzy Wetlaufer Welch come to mind.) Still, given the choice, few people would select a certified poacher as a close confidante or role model for their kids.

How Her Hiding Helps You

Initially, having an illicit affair can seem more exciting than an open relationship, as lovers are preoccupied with their clandestine meetings and their need for secrecy. But as time goes on, the burden of keeping the liaison hidden outweighs the excitement (or, in more scientific terms, the physiological arousal) one feels when doing something dangerous or forbidden. Instead of fostering the allure between the partners, the burden of having to conceal the affair from one's support system becomes a drag on it, eventually reducing relationship satisfaction for the person with the least to hide and the least to lose (typically the unmarried one).

All of the things that normal couples enjoy as their relationship grows and they become more intimate cannot occur when either or both of the individuals must remain mum about their lovers. There is no sharing of family experiences, holidays, celebrations, nothing that publicly ties a couple together in the eyes of their respective kin, clans, or community. Even if one of the affair partners lets a friend or two in on the secret, it's guilty knowledge that often makes the friend feel awkward and uncomfortable, particularly if this person knows the betrayed spouse or family of the married lover.

Lacking the normal progression of enmeshment between a couple's friends and families, not to mention the constant need to stay underground, hidden from the light of day and unfriendly eyes, a secret affair has nowhere to go or grow. If the affair becomes public by dint of your discovery, someone's disclosure, or your husband's confession, the options for all parties are dire. Your husband either breaks off from the affair partner and deals with the severe marital trauma remaining between you; or your husband remains with the affair partner, leaving behind more intense marital trauma for you and often leading to divorce and hurt feelings for you, your kids, and the entire family for many years into the future. In the long run, we are not only dead (as noted by economist John Maynard Keynes), but in the case of an affair, no one wins while living, least of all the affair partner who will forever wear the black hat for breaking up the marriage—*your* marriage, whether she stays or goes.

So, what do you take from this section? If your husband's affair was secret—and most of it is—it's probably a relief for him to finally have the matter out in the open so he can end it and both of you can begin to repair your relationship. If he opts for her, you can make his life as painful or as easy as you (and your lawyer) deem appropriate. In any event, you can be sure that the intense secrecy required to maintain most affairs inhibits, rather than enhances, the quality of an intimate relationship that's supposed to be based upon mutual sharing and commitment. (How does one share what must remain covert? How does one commit when already taken?) And remember, only one in ten affairs will result in a marriage. (The rest just destroy other people's.) Furthermore, of the 10 percent of adulterous affairs that do become marriages, more then 60 percent (some studies suggest the number is closer to 70 percent) of those will end in divorce. Can you say schadenfreude?

Pillow Talking It Out

No matter what's happened before and how you found out about it (or, even if you're not completely certain but you feel that something isn't right), there is no one in a better position than you are to talk with your husband. Whether you are still sleeping together in the same bed or are living in separate rooms or separate states, you remain the one who has the most to say and the most to learn from a dialogue with your spouse. Besides, apart from his attorney or therapist (if he's got either or both), you still have the best access to him (assuming no restraining orders!).

While in the prior section we explored your support-seeking skills, this part will examine the conversation practices that promote frank exchanges and a chance to learn and grow closer after hearing each other's experiences, thoughts, feelings, worries, and perhaps explanations for past behaviors. Plus, as you see in the next section, the ability to communicate is a predicate to handling conflict in a positive, constructive way (a necessary skill for every successful, healthy relationship involving more than one human).

Emotional Expressiveness

In the last chapter we examined various scenarios involving communication when you've just learned that your husband's been involved in an affair. We reviewed how having a rant is generally not productive and if revenge is the motive, you're better off to wait till you cool off, using Houston dentist, Clara Harris, as an example of what not to do.

Here, you're not in the midst of a marital emergency as much as you're beginning the marital repair phase. This is the time when you have the opportunity to begin a dialogue with your husband that can lead you on the road to recovery or, if that's not possible, a better understanding of where you are, how you got there, and where you are headed. Even when it's difficult for you (as you are probably still hurt and angry) to reach out to your husband, if you want to re-establish a rapport with your mate—or take him back—this is the time to bite the bullet. Ask the right questions (How did we get to this point? What did/do you feel you get from her? How do you feel now that I know?) and listen to your husband to help him resolve the situation he created with the affair. Other items high on the must-discuss priority list are how to remove the mate-poacher from his life and how can you both save your marriage.

By implementing the information in this section, you become the active listener, the warm companion—and, if you are prepared, the forgiving partner (covered in the last part of this book). You know from prior chapters that there are different strategies for mate retention than for mate selection. Since you are in mate-keeping mode (as the mate-poacher remains in mate-attraction mode), remember to highlight the qualities that researchers tell us are desirable in a long-term companion (including integrity, honesty, warmth, kindness, dependability, enthusiasm, and carefulness) when you are together for a chat or talking on the phone.

Mars and Venus Revisited

Research tells us that men and women communicate differently. No surprise there. Men tend to be competitive and domineering, while women tend to be cooperative (seeking understanding and consensus) and subordinate. Men and women also differ in the use of questions (and quality of responses to questions) and attitudes towards advice giving and problem-solving. Men's language is generally rule-oriented (dealing with achievement, rules, laws, facts, and abstractions), whereas women's is relationally oriented (dealing with seeking or maintaining interconnectedness). Knowing these general differences will help when you encounter a response that you could otherwise interpret as defensive or hostile. It might just be masculine, without a value judgment attached. No matter your gender role, when you speak with your husband, remember that you are not agreeing with him or forgiving him by giving him your attention and lending your ears.

Marital Conflict: You Can Work It Out

Effective conflict management skills are critical to maintaining a healthy relationship. Perhaps your and your husband's inability to manage disagreement made your relationship vulnerable to outside attack to begin with. If so, you certainly aren't in the minority.

Experts tell us that all discussion, whether it's a casual conversation or deadly serious debate, occurs along a continuum for each person. On one end you have engagement (active participation—positive or negative) and on the other, avoidance (withdrawal). The positive people on the far side of the engaged continuum are the problem-solvers who typically express their experiences, opinions, arguments, and rationales on the issues in contention. At the same time, they consider their partner's positions, feelings, and opinions when seeking a resolution to the conflict by reaching a compromise or influencing their partner to change his mind. The negatively engaged people begin with negative behaviors (criticizing, raging, or blaming) or reciprocate their partner's negative communications and in many cases, take the opportunity to escalate the hostility up a notch, as opposed to deflecting it. Avoiders, on the other end of the scale, tend to be defensive or withdrawn, not offering their opinions or feelings on the matters in contention. Instead of working toward resolution, avoiders will either deny a problem exists or decide to let it go, sweeping it under the carpet. Watch for passive-aggressive behavior or depression among the avoiders who, though unable to verbalize their feelings, are still experiencing them, only without release or opportunity for resolution.

Who's likely to do what? Human beings tend to act according to their past experiences and predictions of the future. In the case of a conflict, scientists found that if a person believes her partner will listen or consider changing a behavior or a position based upon argument, she will be positively engaged, behaving in a way that will produce the possibility of evoking that change. If, on the other hand, a person believes that her partner won't be open to her influence, she will generally either go negative (escalating hostility) or withdraw (disengage), accepting the situation, denying it, or leaving it.

The Gottman Five

John M. Gottman, Ph.D., has devoted many years to studying how couples fight (all do, it's just a matter of how effectively). He has found that the number-one rule for maintaining marital satisfaction, even during times of disagreement, is to engage in five positive behaviors for every negative one. You can criticize, blame, be sarcastic, verbally aggressive, show contempt, shame, belittle, escalate a slight, or dismiss your husband's worth twenty times a day, and you'll have a satisfying marriage so long as you direct at least 100 positive behaviors (complimenting, listening, validating, giving emotional support, facilitating speech, seeking compromise, de-escalating trouble, being affectionate, sharing humor, showing joy, psychologically stroking, and being warm and inviting) toward him during that same period. Why does it take five good acts to make up for one bad one? Because our psyches register bad more deeply than good; it's that simple.

Knowing how to communicate and how to fight well will serve you when dealing with a mate's serious transgression, whether it's extramarital involvement or any other common marital issue pertaining to sex, money, kids, or in-laws. But don't despair if you feel your interactions are primarily negative. In addition to finding a good therapist or support group, where you can work on the problems that underlie the anger and hostility in your marriage (attachment issues, perhaps?), you can work on making your interactions more positive. Meanwhile, couples can improve their interactions by using what Gottman calls "repair mechanisms" (i.e., finding compromise, sharing joy, disclosing feelings—good and bad, but in a respectful way, and de-escalating negativity by a spark of humor or wit, and always seeing the bigger "marital" picture) before the conversation becomes too destructive.

Turning the Tide by Exposing Her Shortcomings

Finally, it's time to discuss the effectiveness of dissing the mistress. ("You were with *her*?" you ask your husband, holding your nose in disbelief.) Before we delve into the dirt of mate-keeping strategies, let's consider the likely facts.

Your work will depend on whether your husband is still involved with the interloper or has agreed to give her up (assuming she wasn't a one-night stand or transgression that's old news and over, though you've just found out). If she's out of the picture, you can satisfy your mate-keeping duty by keeping her out of your marriage. She's over, history. Don't give her psychic space in your marriage.

On the other hand, she might still be very much in the picture, either as the current mistress or the wanna-be. In that case you can be sure that she'll soon lose her patience and develop a strong motivation to dethrone you. (There can only be one wife, notwithstanding HBO's *Big Love* series to the contrary.) In my experience, when the wife remains in the power seat, the other woman becomes more demanding.

Though still lacking any legal status, the fact that she's not been banished after discovery will give her a sense of entitlement. In an effort to take your power and place, she will often resort to making wife-like demands and attempt to exercise wife-like privileges (using your husband's credit cards, insisting on more weekend time or vacations). While this situation might seem awful to you, it's usually to your advantage.

The more she pushes, the more she'll begin to make your husband feel the same pangs of annoyance, irritation, and frustration that might have made him say "yes" to her in the first place. If he wanted to escape your perceived wifely nagging, he's not going to be delighted with hers. This is particularly true if he's been left with only half of his assets, and alimony payments, not to mention loss of daily contact with his kids and the potential of therapy bills for the entire family from now to eternity. You hope she starts in with her demands. From a perfectly ironic and absolutely predictable psychological viewpoint, this is exactly the phase of the mate-poacher's relationship with your husband where you, the betrayed wife, have the best opportunity to regain your position as number one, using your wifely assets to turn the emotional tables around in your favor.

The Battle of Eve Versus Lilith

If the mate-poacher is astute at this stage (after your discovery of her existence), instead of making demands that might annoy your husband, she will continue pretending to have qualities she lacks in an effort to maintain your husband's continued emotional dependence. She knows that the stakes are high because the jig is up. In addition to giving him all the attention and sex he might crave, she will listen to your husband's tales of woe (about you, perhaps, and even his dilemma: her or you) *ad nauseam*. Even if she's not a bit interested in the topic de jour, she will fake it to make him think she's the embodiment of understanding and kindness (though she is not).

If you make the decision to fight for your man, you can become what your husband was looking for in the mate-poacher (someone warmer, more understanding, and mate-centric) in the first place. Increase your mate value—at her expense—by doing what you must to improve your standing to make her suffer by comparison. Meanwhile, you can break the mate-poacher's spell by exposing her flaws. The fact that the other woman is often conceited, selfish, insecure, relationally aggressive, indiscreet, emotionally unstable, vain, self-absorbed, deceitful, acquisitive, cruel, manipulative, controlling, vindictive, and hostile makes her an unattractive life mate, no matter how superficially appealing she might have initially appeared to your husband by being a better friend. By aiming your pointed arrows at the mate-poacher's many Achilles' heels, you can effectively outfox the fox, saving your husband from turning a lamentable, but temporary, marital mistake into a tragic, enduring, lifetime blunder. In the end, your husband may be grateful for your sincere concern and guidance; humbled and chastened, he will generally try to make amends. If she subdued your man by guile, you shall retain him with honesty and opportunity to make your relationship stronger and better.

As the wife, you can win the ultimate marital battle, as your resilience and strength cut through the pain you have suffered. Between you and the other woman, she has the least to lose, and you have the most to gain. Depending upon her psychology and your shrewd wifely moves, she'll either move on to a man with a less attentive wife or fight for her life to hold on to your husband. In that case, you'll be united with your mate against her—in court, no doubt.

CHAPTER 10

Is It Worth the Effort?

Depending on your marriage, your mate, and your mindset, after all things are considered, you might be better off trying to make your relationship work, even after a marital trespasser has appeared, trust is broken, and damage is done. Still, there are types of marital breaches and behaviors that are so egregious and damaging that remaining in the marriage will not bode well for your mental or physical health. In those cases, you will be better off moving on.

Do You Still Want Him?

Let's begin by asking the basic question: What are you willing to live with, and what are you not? It's important to consider all the facts. Unless you've found someone new or are emotionally (and will be financially) autonomous, life after divorce can be more stressful than you ever anticipated.

Actually, the decision to divorce or separate (whether informally by agreement or legally by court decree) might not be up to you. Your husband might have already packed his bags or told you of his intentions to do so in the near future. If you don't agree that immediate physical separation is the best course of action, you will want to do whatever you can to dissuade him from leaving and persuade him to see a couple therapist before he makes a mistake that he could regret for the rest of his life. Once physically separated, couples are less likely to permanently reconcile as they become used to living alone or with another.

Even if his affair is old news to him, it becomes a new shock when *you* find out and your family life as you both knew it is on the line. Neither one of you should be making any rash decisions before the immediate trauma is tended to, the meaning of the betrayal is digested (why it happened, how it happened, whether it's really what he wants), and opportunities for reconciliation have been explored. The same things hold true for filing for divorce. As you'll read about later in this chapter, most no-fault divorce states allow the "bad" spouse (the cheater) to file for divorce as easily as the betrayed spouse. Unless you live in New York (which, as of the date of this printing, continues to be the sole holdout for a fault-based divorce system) or elected a covenant marriage in Arizona, Arkansas, or Louisiana, within the last decade, your wrongdoing mate can file the papers to begin your divorce.

Though acting in haste could be devastating for your family, short of exerting personal influence on your husband to slow it down, there is nothing legal you can do to stop him. But take heart. Though the choice may not be solely yours to dissolve your marriage on account of his cheating, more than two-thirds of all American divorces are filed by women. Therefore, you will probably be the one to decide how your situation is legally resolved.

According to an article in *Journal of Marriage and the Family*, one of the reasons men remain in marriages (yet feel entitled to keep mistresses or cheat on occasion) is that they are globally committed to providing for their families. They feel a sense of financial, community, or religious obligation to stay in the household, even if these duties did not prevent them from straying in the first place. Furthermore, men generally submit to inertia when it comes to relationships matters. An article from *American Law and Economics Review* reports that unless a husband is unhappier in marriage than his wife, he will tend not to be the filer. What's more, sexual dissatisfaction or emasculation (lack of respect, refusal of influence) can motivate a man to file for freedom.

Only you can know how your husband would rate on the happiness scale, but having this information can help you go ahead and gage whether your husband might be the one to pull the legal plug on your marriage or whether that option will be yours. Wives, by the way, are more likely to divorce over specific relational deprivations (no intimacy, no sex, no companionship) or their husbands' bad behavior (cheating, gambling, abusive conduct, and drug or alcohol dependency) than general dissatisfaction.

The Uncoupling Process

Nipping the dissolution process in the bud requires you to be ever vigilant to the pulse of your spouse and your marriage. If you see or sense your partner slipping away, get thee and he to a counselor! If not, we know from clinical and anecdotal evidence that the unhappy spouse will begin to build a single life for himself, slowly but surely, often long before he tells his spouse. By the time he's created a social narrative of himself as single (and a rationale for himself of what went wrong in his marriage) it's usually too late to save the marriage.

Your Mitigating Factors

Wives do divorce husbands on account of their infidelity; substance dependency, abusive behavior, and emotional issues are the top causes. Still, most women will consider mitigating factors before deciding to file the papers. The decision to remain in a marriage damaged by betrayal depends primarily on how committed you are to your spouse, your relationship, and your kids. We know from past chapters that marital commitment is related to individual satisfaction, or the happiness you feel when psychic rewards exceed the punishments—or costs—of a situation. Even if you are personally unhappy, staying in a marriage for the sake of your kids can be rewarding in its own right as long as substance use or abusive conduct are not present. Moreover, while having kids may initially make couples unhappier (and can even precipitate an affair with some husbands), the fact of being parents tends to decrease divorce. You will also assess the availability of attractive alternatives to the living situation and husband you presently enjoy (or suffer), living where—and how—you do.

In addition to assessing personal satisfaction and other opportunities, deciding to divorce involves your social, religious, and ethical beliefs (moral values) about the sanctity of

Six Degrees of Divorce

In 1970, Paul Bohannon wrote of six different stages of divorce (legal, emotional, economic, co-parental, community, and psychic) to help people realize the depth and breadth of the marital dissolution process. No matter how simple you think it will be, the divorce experience is rarely effortless or easy. (If abuse is present, however, it can be a lifesaver.)

marriage, the meaning of family, and your opinion of divorce in general. You are also likely to evaluate the practical aspects of divorcing. These include the future loss of spousal income and company (even mundane aspects, like losing help with kids and performing household chores) before making a leap to singledom. Plus, if you are like many women in your position, you can expect to consider the real costs (money and aggravation) of marriage termination procedures, as well as the personal and capital investments. There will be social alliances, precious human time, and financial security (money, property, pensions) that will be lost—or diminished—if you part.

While weighing the pragmatic sides of divorce, be aware that your self-esteem and personal identity as well as your perception of your husband's betrayal (from bad but understandable under the circumstances to utterly unforgivable—or something in between) will influence your ultimate decision. Naturally, your husband's attitude and demeanor after your discovery of the affair will matter, too. For instance, you'll be evaluating whether he's remorseful and acknowledges responsibility for taking that last step into the void. Or does your husband justify or minimize his transgression? (The latter is not conducive to rebuilding lasting trust, while the former gives you something to work with.)

According to the *Handbook of Divorce and Relationship Dissolution,* a wife is also less likely to end a marriage when a husband provides an unsolicited confession of his affair. This is true regardless of whether the confession was offered in self-preservation, to steal the thunder from an impending news-break from another source, or to put a more positive spin on a bad situation. The wife is more likely to initiate divorce if she discovers her husband's affair herself, if he confesses when she confronts him with her suspicions or evidence, or if she hears of the affair from a third party.

Years of Marriage Make a Difference

Helen Fisher, author of *Why We Love: The Nature and Chemistry of Romantic Love,* reports that the love chemicals operate to make you euphoric for at most four years, more commonly just two.

Is it any wonder that year four of marriage (at approximately the 3.5-year mark) is the most common time for couples to divorce? In fact, researchers studying the subject learned that these early divorces are caused more from a realization that the couple is incompatible in a global sense than any other factor. Once the love high from the chemical cocktail wears off, the couple wonders what in the world they were thinking of. These divorces are typically between people under age thirty-five who are also childless. Anther popular time to file is year twelve or nineteen. These divorces are caused by specific problems, rather then a wake-up realization of being married to the wrong person. These older marriages are the ones where infidelity, growing apart, substance dependency, or abusive behavior are cited as reasons for the split.

In your case, the only thing that matters is what is best for you and your family. Still, it might help you to see where you stand in relation to all the other couples who are considering or filing for divorce, regardless of whether infidelity was a feature of the breakup.

When infidelity is present, we've learned that wives will consider the extent of the offense (whether it's a one-time transgression or a pattern) and will also judge whether their other needs are met by the relationship. As the investment theory predicts, before they file for divorce, wives determine their satisfaction level from the relationship. They judge the degree to which their emotional, psychological, financial, and sexual needs are met, as well as the existence of better prospects outside the marriage.

In many cases, if the infidelity is ongoing, the wife ends the marriage. Yet one study has found some wives become habituated to infidelity and accept the behavior as part of the overall mix. Theoretically, this is because they performed the cost/benefit analysis and for them, it's better to remain married than not. It could also be due to personality (remember the Big Five traits, dependent personality disorder, and insecure attachment problems) that these women choose to remain in destructive marriages, seeing no other way to handle the situation or evaluate their prospects.

While you consider what is right for you (perhaps your husband's profound regret and heartfelt apology), recall that as a woman, your brain chemistry makes you more susceptible to traumatic reactions after stressful events, sometimes long after they have occurred. So, discovery or disclosure of your husband's affair could be having a more devastating effect on your psyche than your husband could ever personally appreciate (lacking your estrogen supply and prolonged cortisol release). Consider allowing him to express his sorrow, focus on what he did and why, and correct his behavior. Don't let your brain chemicals make you do something reflexively that you might regret in the calmer days of quiet reflection ahead.

When Staying Produces More Pain

Some marriages just aren't worth saving. To read about one that, unfortunately for all involved, continued, pick up a copy of Christopher Dickey's memoir, *Summer of Deliverance: A Memoir of Father and Son.* Be sure to savor the part where the author's dad reads an ode to his mistress called "Adultery," in his wife and son's presence, which ends with the line, "God bless you. Guilt is magical."

Exploring Your Options with Pros (Lawyers and Marital Therapists)

Many people on the verge of marital crisis caused by an interloper ask for direction on whom they should meet with first, the therapist or the divorce lawyer? My answer is both, no matter which order. As you know from Chapter 8, a therapist can help you determine whether your marriage is viable (or not), while the lawyer will explain your rights upon divorce. Let's look at the legal aspects now.

Hired Guns and Marriage

Adultery is rarely relevant in a divorce proceeding (unless something lewd occurred in the presence of underage children). The law will not punish your husband for having an affair. Violating marital vows entitles you to a divorce, but it's not necessary to end a marriage. Under no-fault divorce law, any spouse can end a marriage if he or she swears that the marriage needs ending. What began as a movement to spare people the expense of fighting over the reasons why they no longer wanted to be married has left us with a legal system in which each spouse—regardless of fault—can break the marital bond by filing papers saying the partners are incompatible or that the marriage is irreconcilable. The laws of marital dissolution differ from state to state, so see a lawyer licensed in your area to obtain personal, professional advice that pertains to your special situation. For more detailed information, go online to the American Bar Association Family Law site (at *www.abanet. org*) or Lorna Wendt's Equality in Marriage Institute (at *www. equalityinmarriage.org*).

No matter how you feel about the ease with which one can file to end what was supposed to be a lifelong commitment, it's reality, and you have to face what could be your future, like it or not. To get the most out of this situation, you will need legal advice and possibly continued legal representation throughout your divorce. To test the legal waters, make an appointment with an attorney who specializes in family or domestic-relations law. It's best if you can speak with a satisfied client or trusted friend who knows the attorney's work and reputation for excellence and results. To maximize the benefit you derive from your initial attorney consultation, bring all the financial documents you can get your hands on (tax returns, income statements, pay stubs, work contracts, brokerage account statements, loan applications, mortgage statements, deeds, trusts, rental agreements, business papers, household bills, credit card invoices). Your lawyer needs to know about anything pertaining to you, your husband, kids, your family's health, and of course your lifestyle, including all the income and assets and debts and liabilities you know or suspect exists. To see what's important to a court, you can view a legitimate financial disclosure form online at: *www.judiciary.state.nj.us.*

Therapy—His, Yours, Couple

You recall from Chapter 8 that couple counseling can help you when your marriage reaches crisis, usually soon after a partner's infidelity is exposed. Naturally, counseling can continue to help both of you, as a couple, as you seek to repair your relationship, agree to remain ambivalent, or to split. Here, let's talk about you.

Marital counseling is fine, but in some instances individual therapy will be just what the doctor ordered. Couple counseling will address marital goals and focus on the problems that you and your spouse have experienced as a consequence of your former interaction patterns, communications troubles, attitude problems, and perhaps unmet expectations or hidden agendum. Individual therapy, on the other hand, will help you to understand issues that probably plagued you long before you met your spouse. Most individuals marry burdened by all the baggage—good and bad—of their former lives.

If your family of origin was dysfunctional, then your opportunity for learning healthy, non-neurotic behavior was probably limited. Without good examples, it's difficult to know how to be a functional, well-adjusted mate and parent. Naturally, the same is true for your husband. Individual therapy can help you turn your life around, putting an end to the destructive behaviors that have not been effective (though they've been comfortable) to date. In fact, some therapists find that individual therapy can be just as, if not more than, effective as working with the pair in couple counseling. In individual therapy, you can address the emotional dysfunctions that can underlie much of your destructive behavior and ineffective (or harmful) interpersonal interactions and reactions. In cases where a spouse has a personality disorder, individual therapy is nearly always a good idea to help that person understand where her problems originate.

Consider Kate's case. By the time she saw me for individual treatment, Kate was lonely and unhappy with the state of her own life, much less her marriage. I learned that she had been married to John for eight years and had no kids. The preceding year, she had discovered that her husband had an affair during an out-of-town business trip. When she confronted him, he threatened to kill himself and begged her forgiveness, which she granted.

When I asked Kate about her relationship with John, she said when they first dated, she could tell that John was very sensitive and needy—which at the time, she liked. Throughout the relationship, Kate felt the need to protect and comfort John. She noticed that he totally depended on her and had few friends. Moreover, he didn't like Kate to spend any time away from him. He was also moody with a tendency to rage and then beg for her forgiveness. Kate never broached her concerns about John with him, preferring not to invoke one of his violent reactions. Despite what she saw, Kate was in love and ignored her mother's plea that she decline John's proposal of marriage.

After they were married, John's mood swings and rages intensified. Kate had had many friends, but gradually let her friendships slip away because spending time with pals wasn't worth receiving the brunt of John's emotional lashing when she returned. John's mood swings made her house inhospitable, so, over the years, Kate learned how to deal with John's behavior and occupy her interests. She enjoyed the good times and rode out the bad. Kate often felt fortunate that at least she didn't have it as hard as her mother. Kate's father was a moody, angry, anxious, frustrated man, and Kate knew too well how difficult living with him had been on her, her siblings, and her mom.

During individual treatment, Kate discovered that her dad was a diagnosed borderline. Kate gained insight into her own behavior and how, in an unconscious way, she too had selected a borderline for a husband. When Kate pieced it together, she realized how she'd "married" her father when she wed John. She had become her mother without knowing it. Kate also learned how her codependent behavior played a part in her life choices and how she had personal issues, apart from John's, that needed attention.

Around this time, John began treatment to learn how to better manage his depression, anxiety, and rapid mood swings, common symptoms of borderline personality disorder. He made a commitment to continue therapy, fortified with the knowledge that he could do very well with professional help and personal determination. Neither would say that John's one-night-stand had been a good thing, but for them, it served as a vehicle to find a path to live together in a healthier relationship.

In any case, whether you have serious psychological symptoms that require diagnosis and treatment (from talking cures to prescription drugs) or basic insecure attachment issues that make you fear abandonment or avoid intimacy (setting the stage for an affair, perhaps?), a qualified individual therapist can identify your issues and help you overcome the problems they've helped to create in your life.

Examining the Ex Factor

An affair traumatizes marriage. Yet, there are many, many marriages that have undergone painful but positive transformations after an affair rocked them to their very cores. (More on this aspect in Chapter 12.) These marriages are often stronger and healthier after the affair—and all the work that's required to put them back on track—than they were before. By the same token, there are also lots of marriages untouched by infidelity but that are dangerous to remain in due to the conduct involved. These include marriage to a man who is physically, sexually, or emotionally abusive; who uses or abuses drugs or alcohol; or who endangers his family's welfare by intentionally or negligently exposing them to financial ruin (from gambling, illegal activity, or antisocial or thrill/risk seeking behavior). Such marriages almost never end well for a wife and children if the family is not protected and the offending behavior continues.

Infidelity, however, can usher in a new phase of marriage that is cherished and protected by both parties, who know just how close they came to losing their lives together. This is particularly true if the affair was precipitated by a hole in the relationship—a void that you are able to recognize and are motivated to repair. For now, we'll concentrate on the things you should consider whether you are presently calm and philosophical about your husband's affair or whether you are feeling so angry and hurt by his betrayal that your desire for revenge (and his pound of flesh) makes you doubt your ability to ever speak with him civilly, much less as his wife.

Some Divorce Facts to Consider

Your reaction to divorce after your husband's infidelity will differ according to your individual psychological profile, your personality, and the specifics of your relationship and the affair. A study presented in the *Handbook of Divorce and Relationship Dissolution* reported that people who divorce are more depressed, less healthy, and are less satisfied from life than their married counterparts. Moreover, people who divorce on account of infidelity report more distress than those whose divorces did not involve cheating. Studies also found that following divorce, betrayed spouses were more emotionally connected to their exes and less well adjusted to the split than those whose divorces were not caused by infidelity. Of course, infidelity causes a marital crisis whether you divorce or remain married, but I share these facts to let you see that divorce, though superficially an appealing way to deal with the betrayal, may not be the perfect solution for you.

Divorce dissolves the legal bond of your marriage and determines domestic relations issues such as support, property distribution, and parenting time. However, it does not solve the human problems within relationships. Several years ago, Linda J. Waite and her colleagues working for the Institute for American Values, a conservative and promarriage think tank, researched whether divorce made people happier. Their findings: No. Unless there was violence or abuse, which made parting necessary, divorce rarely increased anyone's happiness factor. Rather surprisingly, Waite and her team found that most people who characterized their marriages as "unhappy" but stayed married reclassified those same marriages as "happy" five years later. (Their report is available online, at *www.americanvalues.org.*)

I am not suggesting that you read the Waite report and remain married to a serial womanizer or a husband with a personality disorder who lacks the will to get help to change his behavior. At the same time, I do believe that you should have all the information you need before setting your husband off, free to marry again, if that's not what you really want or what will make your life better. In fact, before my patients make the final decision to divorce, I ask each if she is ready to give up a future with her husband. Is she prepared to let go and watch her mate marry another, who will become the new Mrs., not only replacing the wife (my patient) in all social functions, but who also will become the legal stepmother to her kids? Often, just asking these kinds of questions will give the patient pause, allowing her to reflect on her priorities and whether throwing it all away is really what she wants.

I'll always ask where, when, and how a patient came up with her plan of action after finding out about her husband's affair. If she answers, "from friends," we explore the dynamics of her friends and their own marital situations to evaluate if what they told her was really sound. For instance, in response to friends' advice, "Dump him!" I try to provoke some insight by asking my patient questions to uncover her pals' conscious or unconscious motives, biases, or projections—which could be influencing their advice. (Why do you think Denise Richards told Heather Locklear to dump Richie?)

As a final point, you've probably heard or read about the research on the benefits of close, loving companionship. It can increase how long we live, make us heal faster, and keep us healthier by improving our immune functioning and reducing onset of depression, addictions, and other maladies (probably by increasing our bodies' levels of oxytocin and other protective hormones). On the other hand, an unhappy marriage can harm our health by causing constant tension and the release of cortisol and other stress hormones (like prolactin) that wreak havoc with our immunity and overall well-being. In that light, the issue really becomes this: Can you fix what went wrong that allowed the stranger into your husband's bed, or is the matter hopeless and beyond your repair?

Truly, the only way to find out what went wrong is with work, dedication to the cause (making meaning of what happened; why it happened; what role each spouse played in the drama leading to the triangle; and evaluating whether to go on as intimate lovers and friends), and a willingness to persevere after profound betrayal. Guided perhaps by a wise and knowledgeable therapist, only you will know for sure whether you can forgive your husband and work on the marriage, or if it would be better to call it a day and gain your freedom. Just remember, in some cases (again, not where abuse or addictions are present) Joni Mitchell was right. You don't know what you've got till it's gone. The important message for the moment is simple. Don't make any hasty decisions that while immediately satisfying, will be ultimately detrimental to your long-term well-being.

Part 4

DECIDING HOW YOUR
STORY ENDS

CHAPTER 11

To Your Own Rescue

This last part of the book is devoted to you—as a wife, a woman, and an individual—and how you can best handle the marital storm that either hangs over your horizon or has already arrived full force in your life, bringing winds of change and uncertainty about the future. Fortunately, as a human being you have some experience with your inability to predict or plan for the future with certainty. At any given time, all you can do is your best, moment to moment, making the most of the future, while not worrying about that which you cannot change (the past) or control (the "future" and anyone else of full age and free will). Still, knowing this philosophical approach to life and applying it in trying times are two distinctly different matters.

This chapter will help you put things in perspective, whether you decide to divorce or work through the issues that preceded your marital crisis. Either way, it's perfectly natural for you to be feeling overwhelmed, confused, distraught, and maybe stretched beyond your capacity to cope. Now, let's see how to weather the storm of marital woe (on your own, with a group, or by appealing to the highest power) with the least amount of wear and tear on your body, mind, and spirit. You know that being human means encountering adversity. Unless you are very sheltered (a huge disadvantage in the long run) you will find obstacles, and disappointments. Managing your life's joys and sorrows ultimately makes all the difference.

The Damage of Stress

Hans Selye, an endocrinologist born in 1907, is credited as the first scientist to find that humans suffered physical damage from stress. (Stress is actually a misnomer that entered the popular lexicon because English was not Selye's first language; he later indicated that he would have preferred to use the word "strain.") Dr. Selye developed the famous general adaptation syndrome (GAS) to explain how stress—actually, the physiological process of responding to a stressor—can damage the body instead of protecting it, depending on how the person's system responds.

According to Selye, if stress hormones and neurotransmitters like cortisol remain unchecked, a person will become sick. Common stress-induced conditions include high blood pressure, increased blood sugar and cholesterol, heart disease, muscle weakness, belly fat, bone loss, depressed immunity and healing, assorted gastrointestinal ailments, some cancers and ulcers, and aggravation of viral infections (shingles, herpes) and autoimmune disorders (lupus, MS).

Seeing Clearly and Coping Styles

Now that you know why unmanaged stress is bad for you, how do you try to cope with your stressors—be they financial, marital, emotional, physical, or even existential? According to the experts, you'll assess your stressor. A stressor can be perceived as good or bad. Do you identify the stressor as a threat or a source of harm or loss, or is it more of an opportunity or challenge? Second, you'll consider whether you can effect change (make a difference to the outcome) or not. Your coping style will typically depend upon the answers to these questions. There are three general coping styles: task-focused, emotion-focused, and avoidant-focused.

Task-Focused Coping

Task-focused coping is constructively engaged in solving the external problem or overcoming the challenge posed by the stressor. An example might be finding a good marital therapist, though you are upset and angry at your husband. Task-focused copers will use various strategies, such as seeking information or learning new skills, when attempting to meet the demands of their circumstances. For the most part, task-focused coping or problem-solving is effective when the stressor is something you can control or change.

Emotion-Focused Coping

Emotion-focused coping centers on regulating how you feel when you encounter the stressor. Adjusting the way you react is effective if you cannot change the situation. For instance, if you just discovered that your husband had a one-night stand, you can't change what he did, but you can minimize the event in your mind or seek social support to make you feel better about the distressing event. Or perhaps you would positively reappraise the situation, saying to yourself that your husband learned his lesson and he'll never do it again because he's sorry and admits it wasn't worth betraying your trust and hurting you so deeply.

Avoidant-Focused Coping

Finally, avoidant-focused coping involves making a conscious decision not to employ any strategy at all to deal with the stressor. Escapism via daydreaming or magical thinking is a common avoidant tactic. Coping strategies differ depending upon the stressor and an individual's own resources (personal, capital, social, or spiritual). Most experts believe that people employ a combination of these coping styles to meet the environmental or internal demands the stressor produces. No matter which style you use, the past can't be changed, but the future is always open, depending on your life view and what you choose to do.

Coping Is Conscious

Don't confuse coping with denial. Choosing a problem-solving strategy is conscious, even if you choose to be avoidant. On the other hand, defense mechanisms are unconscious and are used to repress or deny material to protect the conscious ego from psychic pain or discomfort. Sometimes, avoidant-focused coping is appropriate, but denial or repression will usually get you into trouble.

On a short-term basis, denial is a blessing. On a long-term basis, it impedes the ability to go forward and make a plan of action, or grieve, or go on with life.

Mending the Psyche

Even if you are an exemplary at coping, you still might be feeling depressed, down, or despairing over how things are going—or how they are not. The best antidote against negativism is keeping your mind on the present tasks and your vision toward the future. Eleanor Roosevelt once said, "No one can make you feel inferior without your consent," and from a psychological point of view, she was on target and emotionally focused. One of the most effective ways to deal with difficult emotions and distressing events (besides seeing a good shrink or therapist) is to write in a journal, read it, review it, and revise it.

According to those who study and practice expressive emotions therapy, individuals who disclose traumatic experiences and feelings in written, narrative form using "cognitive processing" (that is, thinking about the experiences and feelings that they are expressing) fare better, both physically and emotionally, than those who don't. Besides, journaling is cheap, effective, and as private or as public (as in blogging) as you want it to be. Just be careful of slander and privacy laws. Though truth is an absolute defense, most states limit your right to disclose private information to the world without a really good reason, so be careful what you say about the poacher—or your husband—in public. As for your private diary, or a letter to the poacher, go for it. But keep it aside a day, so you can reread it before dispatch. The written word lasts forever; the spoken word can be lost in the ether or forgotten over time.

Another way of making yourself feel better is by taking on a creative project: painting, a poem, a book, whatever. Do not allow guilt, shame, pride, or embarrassment to rob you of an opportunity for growth and development. One famous example of a woman who took a sad marriage and made it better is Anne Morrow Lindbergh. She is said to have begun her classic

A Little Help from Your Pals

No matter whether you stay with your husband or not, support groups or group therapy can be a source of strength and encouragement when you think you are alone and could benefit from other's experience and wisdom. The bonding among members and other group dynamics (transference, empathy, sympathy, reality-testing, and role playing) can promote a unique sense of well-being, strength, and connectedness in times of indecision and marital trouble.

1955 book, *Gift from the Sea*, to write herself out of her marriage, but instead she wrote herself back into it. One of her pearls of wisdom: "The cure for loneliness is solitude." While that might be true in some circumstances, most people do benefit from social support. Just knowing that others care for you, value you, and will help you through a tough time will ease your troubles.

The Highest Power Can Help

Coping with stressors—on your own, with a pen, or with the help of a therapist—or within support groups composed of people in similar situations can be effective and helpful. There are, however, times when life seems overwhelming and something more is needed. In their darkest hours of doubt and despair, many people find peace from their faith or spiritual beliefs. Though praying and seeking succor from a higher source might seem useless to the nondevout, studies reveal that appealing to God or one's faith in times of uncertainty and crisis have a discernibly healing effect on many individuals (and may actually help keep families together).

Much has been written about the health and well-being of the religious or spiritual among us. Research suggests that faith in God or a supernatural power can assist a person's healing and actually reduce emotional distress. Some results, however, show us that using religion or God in the coping process can be harmful. Data on the process of negative religious coping suggests that overall distress increases if in the midst of her crisis, a person believes that her God has forsaken or abandoned her or is punishing her for past sins.

On the other hand, positive religious coping is helpful. For instance, studies reveal that people in distress are helped by turning to religion or God if they believe that the source is benevolent and loving versus condemning and vengeful.

Apparently, those who believe in the judgmental, punishing Yahweh of the Old Testament do not cope as well in resorting to their faith as those who invoke the kinder, gentler Jesus of the New Testament.

Studies have also found that there's a difference in the way people use their religion. People whose religiosity was extrinsic, or generated by outside forces as a means to other selfish ends (such as receiving divine protection or a social life created by church functions), are less likely to benefit emotionally from their beliefs in times of stress. On the other hand, those who are intrinsically religious use their faith as an end in itself to meet personal needs (like comfort from ritual, prayers, or services), regardless of social pressure. For an excellent, detailed exegesis of how religion can add or detract from a person's ability to cope with trauma, pick up a copy of Kenneth Pargament's book, *The Psychology of Religion and Coping: Theory, Research, Practice.*

This is what we know about coping and personal coping processes. Pleading to have God save you or spare you or curse your husband is not effective and will contribute more to your distress than help to alleviate it. Blaming yourself (any past conduct that you believe warrants punishment) or God for your troubles or current plight isn't helpful either. On the other hand, Ben Franklin's maxim "God helps those who help themselves" and the general proverb "God doesn't give you more than you can handle" both fit the mold of positive religious coping.

Seeking purpose and coherence in your current circumstances (by asking yourself why you bear this burden at this time; what lessons you are meant to learn from this; and how can you use what you've learned to help others who will suffer the same fate) is associated with positive coping. Believing that some good can come from a difficult experience generally reduces distress and strain. Moreover, using your spiritual beliefs or religious faith to find connection to something bigger than yourself, thereby transcending your personal, painful present and thrusting yourself into causes, concerns, and duties to others, is sure to help lift your spirits, regardless of your religious attitudes.

Depression Management

Now that you know the ways you can cope with stressors and manage strain, beware of exhaustion. Make sure you rest, eat right, and do what you can to take care of your mind, body, and spirit as you sort out your life and your marriage. Try not to fall prey to the lure of self-medication. Drinking or eating to excess, drugging at all, and being angry and hostile will ultimately cause more distress than the immediate relief they seem to provide. Pay attention to the daily needs of life (sleeping, socializing, eating moderately, and moving your body parts) and the living (caring for those who love and depend on you). After all, living well and taking care of yourself is crucial for your ability to cope. Try exercising to manage stress and release endorphins. Also consider destressing alternatives: bio-feedback, meditation, controlled breathing, dreamwork, progressive muscle relaxation techniques, hypnosis, positive imagery, Pilates, stretching, and yoga. I often suggest taking at least one hour a day to do something just for yourself—without pressure. It may be a long bath, calling a friend, window shopping, or listening to a favorite CD. It may be just giving yourself permission to do nothing without feeling bad about it.

If neither exercise nor stress reduction techniques helps you, ask your doctor if he thinks you could benefit from natural, adrenal-gland friendly supplements like royal bee jelly (an excellent source of pantothenic acid), licorice (in moderation and only under the supervision of a physician), borage oil, kelp, or parsley. If you are feeling more than just blue, get yourself evaluated for depression. There are doctors, therapists, and effective medications—like selective serotonin reuptake inhibitors (SSRIs) or serotonin-norepinephrine reuptake inhibitors (SNRIs)—that can alleviate your suffering. (For more detailed information, go online to *www.depression.com*, a Web site with good information, tests, and resources.) While what you are going through is painful and seems like it will never go away, it will—with help. And though you might not think so at the time, you will survive and eventually thrive. There are better days ahead. Your job is to maintain yourself to meet your future.

CHAPTER 12

Dealing with Trauma and Finding Forgiveness

This chapter explores how and why serenity and contentment are attainable, even after your marriage has been rocked to its foundations. In the end, you will understand why your best bet for health and peace of mind requires you to make final peace with the past.

Toward the New

In order to fully reconcile after crisis-inducing marital infidelity, you must be mindful of the old interactions that made the marriage vulnerable to an affair in the first place. At the same time, you must also move on, psychologically speaking, putting the mate-poacher far behind you.

Understanding the truth behind the aphorism "Forgiving is human, forgetting—divine," I urge you to find the goddess within and retain the lessons you've learned from the experience of coping with your marital crisis. If you decide to stay together, it's best to release any lingering hostility, sadness, resentment, anger, or ill will (feelings that should have been worked out by now, before making the decision to remain married) toward your husband. In the same vein, you must forgive yourself as well for your part in the decline and fall of your marriage knowing that you have the insight, the motivation, and the skills to do better this time around.

Consider relationships in which the husband was unfaithful, yet the wife elected to hang in there for herself, for her family, for her husband. Who could forget the case of Kathy Lee and Frank Gifford? They opted to remain married despite Frank's excruciatingly public 1997 indiscretion with a then-forty-six-year-old married former flight attendant. There are many famous couples (not to mention millions of private folks) who opted to stay together, notwithstanding reports of alleged adultery—or worse.

Unions that have continued in spite of the husband's alleged or proven infidelity should not surprise you. Adapting Nietzsche, what did not kill these marriages must have made them stronger. Or, after all the pros and cons were weighed, the wife in each case was prepared to live within the marriage rather than give it up on account of an interloper. With fewer than 10 percent of affairs ever resulting in a marriage, and with more than 60 percent of those few marriages ending in divorce, why not give your guy a second look (barring abuse, addiction, or criminal behavior)?

According to love professor Dorothy Tennov, affairs occur when temptation overwhelms resistance at a critical moment, and in that light, keeping your marriage for your own selfish reasons can seem sensible and practical. Moreover, as Carol Lloyd reports in her Salon.com article "I Want You So Bad," 80 percent of those who parted due to infidelity regretted their divorce, both the betrayer and betrayed. Remaining in a marriage despite a trauma of betrayal may not be so unreasonable after all.

Finally, Dr. Samuel Johnson famously said, "A second marriage is the triumph of hope over experience." Deciding to reunite after betrayal (or a close call) is not technically a second marriage. Still, you are taking a second chance on commitment, albeit with the same spouse. In many instances, a couple that makes it through the trauma caused by an affair (or a would-be poacher) becomes enormously protective of their bond, the new one that they've forged after having to fight for it. These spouses, tried—and now true—to each other, know that they could have lost all that they ever had as a couple. Coming so close to the end, they diligently tend their union, long after the memory of the intruder has faded away. For many reconcilers, the poacher was the wake-up call to get back on the right track and renew their married lives.

A New Beginning, Either Way

Virgil might have claimed that love conquered all, but when you are talking about living well, what you really need is forgiveness or the ability to move on without harbouring hostility and resentment—both notorious health killers. In this final section, we'll examine the psychological dynamics of forgiveness, what it offers, and why.

The experts who study forgiveness figure it's a relationship repair mechanism that's been in our emotional repertoire for as long as humans have been hurting the ones they love. But before there is forgiveness, there must be a transgression—that is, a deliberate act or omission that is objectively wrong and harms another, physically or emotionally. Just as the law doesn't hold people accountable for accidents, forgiveness is unnecessary (though remorse may arise) if the act or omission was unforeseeable, unintended, or the result of fate. So, identifying the wrong and the wrongdoer is the first step before one even considers forgiveness. Since this is a book about protecting your man and your marriage, let's use your husband's affair as the forgiveness qualifying transgression. (It meets the test of intentional, unacceptable, and wrong.)

Forgiveness can mean different things to many people. In psychological circles, forgiveness is a process. The victim deliberately decides to release the negative feelings (anger, hurt, and resentment) caused by the transgressor's actions and to hold a more positive view of the transgressor. At the same time, she makes it perfectly clear to him that his actions were—and remain—painful, unacceptable, and intolerable. Once the victim decides to forgive the transgressor, she no longer bears him ill will and releases her desires for vengeance or retaliation against him for the wrong committed against her. Forgiveness, you see, is all about the victim and her feelings, not the transgressor or his. According to Frank Fincham, "forgiveness occurs in full knowledge that the transgressor is responsible for the injury, that he or she thereby forfeits any right to the victim's sympathy, affection or trust, and that the victim has a right to feel resentful." So you see, forgiveness is a gift the victim can bestow, or not, upon the transgressor.

Before we dive in deeper, it might help to distinguish what is *not* forgiveness. Adapting is not forgiveness. With forgiveness, you are not sending the message that what the transgressor

The Power of Three   According to other researchers, forgiveness can provide the victim with three things: a clear view of the marriage as it really is; a way to restore her power by ridding herself of the devastating effects from negative emotions held about her spouse; and a diminished need to punish or seek revenge from the spouse.

did was tolerable or something to accommodate, justify, or excuse. Similarly, condoning and excusing are not forgiveness. Living in denial or avoiding the pain of the transgression is not forgiving either. Pardon from a third party (like a judge or the president) is not forgiveness; neither is forgetting, reuniting, or reconciling. You might reunite for a host of practical reasons (such as loneliness, emotional or financial dependence, lack of attractive alternatives, or a lack of power or parity in the relationship), none of which smacks of forgiveness. Reconciliation, while requiring the victim to forgive, also requires the transgressor to act contritely and seek "conciliation" or appeasement from the victim, who is free to accept or deny the effort. Forgiveness, on the other hand, is the victim's sole business. She can opt for it, or not. If it's forced, it's not forgiveness; it's coercion or accommodation.

Why Forgive?

Why forgive your husband's betrayal? The primary reason is to help you feel better or to restore the relationship with your husband by letting him know that what he did was inexcusable, unacceptable, and painful, but that for your sake, you are willing to try to stop ruminating over the offense and dreaming of revenge. You are also ready to release the anger, aggression, hostility, and dudgeon that his offense stirred in you.

In the Jewish faith, forgiveness requires the transgressor to take action. To rid himself of guilt he must offer the victim compensation and seek her forgiveness. The notion of earning forgiveness by action is captured by the Hebrew work *Teshuvah,* whose root means "return." On the other hand, the Christian faith holds that forgiveness is in the hands of the wronged, not the wrongdoer. Fincham points out that St. Augustine's motto, "love the sinner, hate the sin," underscores that nearly all of us are imperfect human beings. Despite having done bad deeds, we might have many other good qualities (such as being a good dad, an excellent provider, generous, or admirable in other matters) that can offset mistakes made—even grave ones. In other words, "Don't throw out the baby with the bath water." (Of course, you can recall more august dictums, like "There but for the grace of God go I" and "Who among you can cast the first stone?" to ease you into the forgiving mood, if that's your bent.) The point is, while your husband's affair is painful, it might not be the right reason to end your marriage.

If your partner is contrite and promises that his behavior will change, forgiving is easier than if he remains unrepentant. If he is unapologetic, you can still choose to bestow forgiveness on him to release the negative emotions you suffer as a consequence of his affair. To forgive, however, does not mean that you deny what happened to you or leave yourself vulnerable to more pain. That would be dumb. If you forgive someone who you know is likely to hurt you again, you are best to forgive for your sake. (This is important to rid yourself of debilitating anger, depression, hostility, rage—they take a toll on *your* health, not your husband's and not the poacher's.) Next, take the steps to eliminate that person from your life, or at least remove him from any position where he could hurt you again. At the end of the day, forgiving allows you to process the negative feelings, get rid of them, and move on. Whether that moving on will be with or without your mate is up to you—and him.

The Positive and Negatives of Forgiving

Scholars say that forgiveness involves not only an absence of bad feelings (thinking the worst of the transgressor and wanting to avoid him or retaliate against him in some way) but that it also includes positive feelings, such as benevolence and a desire to approach. Much has been studied about the positive aspects of forgiveness. Remember the Big Five (discussed on page 99)?

Well, being agreeable and having low neuroticism scores promotes your likelihood of forgiving. (Narcissists rarely forgive, whereas codependents tend to excuse or deny the bad behavior and adapt to the circumstances.) Moreover, not surprisingly, studies show that the better your marriage—the more intimate and satisfied you are with your mate and invested in and committed to your union—the more likely you will be disposed toward feelings of empathy after processing any transgression. Whether you make it to forgiveness or not will depend on the severity of the offense and whether it's an isolated event or a pattern of hurtful behavior. But if you are otherwise happily married, you're on your way.

Interestingly, the negative emotions that a victim suffers upon transgression, such as anger and the drive to retaliate and seek revenge, serve a purpose: to restore a destabilized self-view. Your self-image might have been damaged by your husband's affair and the fact that he didn't think enough of you or your marriage to maintain his vows and keep his zipper closed. In that case, it would be natural for you to want to re-establish your sense of self by taking vengeance on your spouse. Furthermore, if you tend to cherish your rage and are given to fury and rumination, your forgiveness outlook is dim. While holding on to your dudgeon might seem satisfying, nursing hostility over time could cause you to suffer hypertension, compromised immunity, and social isolation, none of which makes for a happy or healthy human.

Consider Sue's story. Sue had known her husband, Jim, since college. They still shared the same bed and enjoyed their children and Sue's success. Sue owned the largest travel agency in the state, servicing huge commercial clients. Though not as financially productive as his wife, Jim did well working for a mortgage broker in the city. He was friendly and outgoing and always eager to help the underdogs of the world.

When it came to helping, Jim sometimes became too involved in the personal lives of the people he helped. There was never a problem, however, till a typist named Tess requested to work for Jim.

Every day, Tess told Jim how smart he was, how handsome he looked, and how she thought he was the best broker in the firm. Jim liked the accolades and sensed no threat from Tess, since she was in her mid-thirties and married with a husband and children at home. Though thinner, Tess was not nearly as good looking, polished, or educated as Sue. In short, Tess was not anyone Jim would ever take a second look at. Still, Jim found himself enjoying and even looking forward to his daily shot of adoration from Tess.

Soon, Tess was giving little gifts to Jim for his office. He was not comfortable with this, but he did not want to hurt her feelings and so simply said thank you and accepted the tokens. More gestures followed and, eventually, Tess became Jim's lover. In his own distorted way, Jim felt that if he confined the affair to work, never taking time from his personal life or his very busy wife, then he wasn't being a bad guy. Plus, since Tess was married, Jim felt she'd never cause much of a problem for him.

Sue's awakening occurred when Tess sent a love note to their house. Shocked, Sue demanded that Jim tell her what was going on. Jim confessed all. They had just celebrated their tenth wedding anniversary, and Jim had given Sue a porcelain figurine of a bridal couple dancing. They both loved it and kept it in their bedroom. In an act of rage, Sue went upstairs to the bedroom, grabbed the figurine, and threw it against the wall, smashing it into many pieces. After that, she went downstairs, got a hammer, walked outside to Jim's beloved Porsche Carrera GT (her anniversary gift to him), and began to strike it over and over. Jim was so stunned at Sue's behavior that he watched her, never once trying to stop her, much less call the police.

When Sue re-entered the house, Jim said that he deserved that and then asked if she was finished. If she was, he wanted to talk. Sue said she was not finished and suggested he not fall asleep in her presence because she could not be held responsible for what might happen to him. He did not sleep that night but did climb into bed with his wife. Sue would not let him touch her, but let him keep vigil and got a good night's sleep.

Sue called me the following week. After a few sessions, it seemed that though she was furious at Jim and hurt by his actions, Sue still loved her husband and had difficulty thinking about a life without him. Sue was still angry for months, but she felt relief when she gained insight into the dynamics that could have precipitated the affair. Sue learned that Jim felt he had lost his place in the marriage and that Sue didn't need him. He also felt resentful of Sue's great success, which in turn, made him feel guilty—none of which he ever articulated. So, feeling useless and inadequate, and then resentful and guilty, Jim fell easily into the arms and charms of the simple, unthreatening Tess.

Sue was able to understand Jim's position and took some responsibility for their situation. Jim and Sue continued treatment for about a year working on restoration of trust and forgiveness (which in Sue's case was preceded by détente). In the end, Sue survived the storm and forgave her husband. Jim is now in the process of considering joining Sue in the travel business.

While there is never an excuse to cheat, there are often many reasons. Learning why your spouse betrayed his vows to you provides you an opportunity to change the tenor of your relationship, as you grow and gain insight from the past. If you played a part, consciously or not, in the breakdown of your marital relationship to the point that an intruder became—or was about to become—involved, now is the time to resolve your actions and forgive yourself. With rare exception (such as a husband with a personality disorder or an addiction) it takes, as they say, two to tango. Find a way to move beyond the pain and the emotional debt you think you are owed and instead concentrate on the things that you can control in life: your actions and reactions. While it is true that forgiveness can take time, be mindful of what Confucius said: "If you dedicate your life to looking for revenge; first, dig two graves."

CHAPTER 13

Potential Costs of Adultery— Regardless

In his *Nicomachaean Ethics,* Aristotle proclaims that "adultery, theft, and murder" are bad actions that never "have a right time or manner." Having just covered forgiveness and moving on (regardless of your husband's bad actions, or whether you decide to remain married to him or not), here you'll see what happens when bad actions result in big trouble for you and your family, even after your immediate marital crisis abates.

While this is not a book about divorce per se, as you'll see, this chapter explores the widespread damage that could arise from your mate's affair—or even flirtation—with a spiteful, disappointed, bitter person—particularly if he doesn't leave you for her.

Before we start, to set the mood, consider the words of William Congreve from *The Mourning Bride,* "Heav'n has no Rage, like Love to Hatred turn'd, Nor Hell a Fury, like a Woman scorn'd." What's more, the linguistic history of the word "adultery" will give you a preview of the material you are about to read. The root of the word adultery is the Latin *adulterare,* meaning to contaminate or pollute by mixing or debasing or fastening to. Think about the English word "adulterate" and you'll get the idea. Now, let us delve into the abyss that can be created by the interloper with an ax to grind.

Emotional Blackmail

Typically, exposing the affair to you (the wife) is the most common of the interloper's threats. In exchange for her forbearance, she often exacts promises from her target (your husband) to do or not do certain things ranging from giving her money to getting her jobs. Some would call her conduct extortion. When the costs become too high, or the affair becomes impossible to hide, either she will make a call and reveal the affair to you (then she becomes your husband's enemy, as she's betrayed her secret role in the affair) or your husband will head her off and confess. Either way, you and your husband lose, while the poacher sits on the side, watching the melodrama unfold.

Claims and Charges

To heck with just telling you, private citizen wife, about the affair or alleged relationship with your husband; the mate-poacher can do something potentially far more damaging to you both. She can elect to file a complaint with your husband's employer or an administrative agency alleging that he sexually harassed her or subjected her to a hostile work environment. Remember the movie *Disclosure,* in which it was the man's (Michael Douglas) word against the female boss played by Demi Moore? If your husband is a business executive, doctor, therapist, judge, or any other kind of public official or fiduciary, a sexual harassment complaint could result not only in a private mess between the two of you and among him and his colleagues, but a public event as well, ending with a formal reprimand, license suspension, or worse: removal from office or professional practice.

Sometimes, the mistress (or mistress wanna-be) isn't the one who makes the report of harassment or foul play. Rather, her friends, foes, or coworkers might not like what they see or are subjected to on account of the hanky panky, and they decide to take action. Remember, it wasn't Ms. Lewinsky who made trouble for President Clinton; Linda Tripp was the one who taped Monica's phone conversations about her dalliances with the president. Similarly, in March of 2005, Harry Stonecipher was fired from his post as CEO of Boeing for violating the company's ethics rules after admitting he'd been having an affair with Debra Peabody, a divorced Boeing executive. The story broke when a female employee—not Ms. Peabody—saw romantic messages between the lovers and notified the Boeing board. Likewise, television host Maury Povich (Connie Chung's husband) didn't personally harass one of his show's associate producers, but that didn't stop her from filing a suit against Maury's producers, citing a hostile work environment and alleging that Maury was having a longtime affair with his producer. (Maury and Connie are together and plan to fight the suit.)

And as bad as these intercompany claims or civil sexual harassment charges can be, it can get worse. The disgruntled mate-poacher or mistress wanna-be can press criminal charges against your husband for anything from stalking her to sexual assault. At this point, the affair goes beyond its personal effect on you and your family, the threat to your marriage, or your husband's reputation and career. By making the matter a criminal case, she puts your mate's liberty at stake.

Uncivil Civil Affairs

In addition to filing harassment claims at work or criminal charges at police headquarters, the poacher can sue your husband in civil court for money damages for a variety of offenses, including these:

- Negligent or intentional conduct—essentially the same conduct as could be alleged in a criminal matter, anything from false imprisonment to sexual assault and battery
- Conduct that while not criminal, breached a duty of care and caused her damage (such as financial loss, emotional anguish, or the contraction of a sexually transmitted disease)
- Fraudulent misrepresentation or breach of implied or express contract (alleging that he promised to marry or support her—think "palimony"—or give her property in exchange for her company or confidence)

For instance, when NBA star Michael Jordan didn't pay his alleged mistress the millions of dollars she believed he owed her upon his retirement from basketball, she sued him.

Ex-lovers certainly file these suits to make money and seek fifteen minutes of fame, but sometimes they also act out of sheer spite, to punish their lovers for leaving them or for staying with their wives. Whatever their motives for filing—greed, extortion, or payback—once these civil suits are made part of the public record, the damage is done, regardless of whether they are eventually dismissed, settled, or tried, with a jury or judge deciding the outcome. Then, it's over—pending appeal, of course. The next section, however, examines the type of suits that look not for closure but rather cash and permanent affiliation.

Paternity Is Forever

Perhaps one of the most damaging effects of your husband's affair is when the mate-poacher becomes pregnant, has a child—or children—and sues your husband for paternity. If DNA proves that your spouse is the father, the court will order him to pay child support to the mother until each child is emancipated, which, depending upon where you live, could be graduation from high school, college, or even graduate school.

As an example of a worst-case scenario, let's review what happened in the 2004 New York custody case involving a middle-aged former model/actress mistress, Ms. Bridget Marks, and an even older, long-married casino executive, John Aylsworth. According to court papers, Bridget and John began an affair in 1998. Bridget learned she was pregnant in 1999. John told his wife of thirty years about the predicament. The wife contacted Bridget and asked her to have an abortion, but Bridget refused. Instead, Bridget bore twin girls, Amber and Scarlet Aylsworth, in September 1999. Bridget and John continued their affair and though the wife filed for divorce in California, she didn't proceed with the action, deciding after the terrorist attacks of September 11 to remain married to John. They were still married throughout the litigation.

This case would not have been so unusual had Bridget not taken the low road of coaching the kids to lie about being sexually abused by their dad during court-supervised visits. As a result of her actions, the New York court ordered Bridget to turn physical custody of the twins over to their dad and his wife, who were ordered to live within forty miles of Bridget's residence in Manhattan. The girls lived with their dad and stepmom for nearly ten months until an appellate court allowed Bridget to regain custody of the twins.

What does this case teach you? First, your husband's affair can have a lifelong effect on your family—emotionally, financially, and physically—by adding new members to his paternal progeny, who by their conception become living testaments to his betrayal. Second, if your husband becomes involved with someone who is "narcissistic and delusional," as Bridget Marks was described by the court-appointed forensic psychiatrist, major problems might await you. Not only did Bridget alleg-edly mislead her lover about using contraceptives during the early days of their affair, she went on to expose her lover to potentially devastating, yet false, charges of child sexual abuse. If John had lacked the resources to defend himself, he may have been found guilty of the sex charges and served prison time. He would also have been permanently registered as a child sex offender, all because his ex-mistress had "unbridled anger" toward him, according to the trial court. For more information about this case, go online to *www.nydailynews.com/front/story/ 203761p-175836c.html.*

Though the Marks case was unusual because of the players involved—and because the father and his long-suffering wife gained custody of the "love twins"—impregnating a mistress is not as uncommon as you'd hope. Famously, Congressman Dan Burton admitted in 1998 that he had a child born of an affair. Burton explained that it happened in the 1980s and that all par-ties concerned, his wife, the mistress, and the son "all reached an agreement." Similarly, Al Pirro, husband of TV commenta-tor and former Westchester County District Attorney, Jeanine Pirro, fathered an illegitimate daughter; yet the Pirro marriage continued. (For more on Ms. Pirro's marital woes, log on to: *www.wnbc.com/politics/9948517/detail.html.*) So, while it can-not be easy, it is possible to remain married despite the dev-astation of learning that your husband fathered a child with another woman. This happens more than you might think, but it doesn't have to be the end of your marriage.

Here's an example of how one of my patients handled the issue. Marilyn was a teacher, married for seven years. Though she loved kids, so far she had none. Her husband Mike was in the military. He had a tour of duty in the Gulf and returned home despondent and different. He went to a counselor and seemed to improve.

Soon after, a woman rang their bell with a young child in tow, announcing that Mike was the father. The woman explained how the child's mother had asked her to find Mike and deliver his son to him so that the boy would have a better life. Marilyn, home alone at the time, called her husband. Marilyn was sure this woman had made a mistake and that Mike would take care of it. Waiting for Mike, Marilyn could not help noticing that the boy did resemble Mike. Her husband was fair with blue eyes, and though this boy was darker skinned, he had the same blue eyes.

Mike came home and looked at the boy and his custodian, whom he'd never seen before. Though he never had any awareness that he had a son, he felt the boy was his. Without thinking, he hugged the child. Marilyn was in shock and couldn't believe what was happening. She invited the woman to bring the child inside the house. She asked Mike to get some milk and snacks for the boy. He nodded to Marilyn and began to say he was sorry. She told Mike they would talk later.

Later, Mike begged for Marilyn's forgiveness, explaining his lonely nights while overseas, missing her and falling to temptation under severely stressful conditions. Mike said that he spent a few nights with a female soldier more to release energy than anything else. But the event meant nothing to him, and the woman never mentioned anything about being pregnant. He never heard from her again and never gave her a second thought. He reaffirmed to Marilyn that he loved her and was deeply sorry and ashamed for not being true when she deserved better from him.

In therapy, Marilyn realized that not being the mother of Mike's child made her angrier than the fact that he had engaged in sex when he was lonely, fearful of dying, and more than half a world away from her and his family. Marilyn agreed to let the child remain with them until they were assured by blood tests that Mike was really the father. In the meantime, the boy won Marilyn's heart. Once the results confirmed Mike's paternity, it took little time for Marilyn to decide she wanted to adopt the boy as hers. They hired a lawyer to finalize their informal custodial arrangement. Marilyn now feels that this child was meant for her, realizing that you don't have to physically bear a child to mother him. Mike is grateful for his wife's forgiveness and grace under the circumstances that could have ended their marriage, and is devoted to her and their boy. He and Marilyn would still love to have child together, but they are content for now to lavish their love on their new son.

The Scarlet Letter Lives

Forget about Hester Prynne, how about Nellie Mae Hensley? She's the fifty-something-year-old mistress who filed adultery charges against her former lover, a married man named John Raymond Bushey, Jr. While nothing happened to Ms. Hensley, Mr. Bushey resigned from his town attorney position and pled guilty to the low-level misdemeanor charge of adultery, which carried a maximum fine of $250. Interestingly, though adultery no longer matters much in divorce law (unless circumstances are extreme, such as funneling marital or community funds through a mistress, or acting lewdly and harming a child), nearly half of U.S. states carry criminal laws on their books prohibiting adultery.

Ms. Hensley's use of Virginia's adultery statute in 2003, though unusual, shows that a mistress can do more than just threaten a marriage. In Mr. Bushey's case, it cost him his job, but not Cindy, his wife of eighteen years, who told reporters that she planned to remain married. So beware the jilted lover. She might not be able to get you to divorce your husband, but she can, as Ms. Hensley proved, charge him with adultery, even if she was the consenting sexual partner in crime.

Similarly, if your husband is in the military, watch out. Instead of facing a fourth-degree misdemeanor charge and a maximum $250 fine, like Mr. Bushey, your husband could be confronting a court-martial on an adultery charge. If convicted, he risks a reduction in rank, loss of pension, removal from command, or dishonorable discharge (or all of the above). Much like a criminal adultery charge, a military adultery charge can be, and is often, brought by the lover's jilted spouse, the lover him/herself, or his/her family. A long-term wife will typically not play the adultery angle, as she could suffer severe economic losses if her husband were found guilty.

In Death Do They Sue

As we briefly discussed in Chapter 3, when talking about lifers and flingers, there are certain mistresses who will keep a very low or invisible profile till your husband dies. Then she will circle the corpse to make sure she receives what she believes she's entitled to by virtue of some secret agreement. Alternately, you find out that she is mentioned in your husband's will (the one signed after you left the lawyer's office) and is set to receive real property or gifts that you thought would be yours or your family's upon his death.

Again, while not an everyday occurrence, having a lifer show up at the lawyer's office after a husband's funeral is not as rare as you'd think. Charles Kuralt's mistress, Ms. Patricia Elizabeth Shannon, kept their affair a secret for twenty-nine years until Charles died in 1997. Then she contested his will. Till that time, Kuralt's widow, "Petie," had no knowledge of Ms. Shannon or her relationship with Charles.

For years, Ms. Shannon fought for her right to receive the ninety-acre Big Hole River estate she and Kuralt secretly enjoyed while the *On the Road* reporter was off the road with her and her kids. Based upon Kuralt's 1989 holographic (handwritten) will and a letter (later ruled a "codicil") written shortly before he died, in which he expressed his desire to leave the disputed parcel to his mistress, the Supreme Court of Montana eventually ruled in her favor. To add insult to injury, not only did the Montana mistress get the land, the Kuralt estate had to pay the substantial estate tax bill caused by the court-ordered property distribution. (You can find the 2003 decision online at *www.lawlibrary.state.mt.us*.)

Your Rights Against Her

Now that you know what the mistress or third parties can do to you or your husband after contact or an affair, it's time to explore your rights against the interloper who either won't go away, or who did—and took your husband with her.

Protective Measures

If your husband's mistress or admirer goes "fatal attraction" on you, you're within your rights to obtain protection via court order (a protective or restraining order). While this is not a common problem, if your husband became involved or somehow encouraged (even without meaning to) a woman who is mentally unstable or who suffers from a personality disorder (as described in Chapter 4), you could be dealing with someone stuck in obsession mode and who doesn't give up or doesn't understand the meaning of "it's over."

If you are unable to communicate to the woman that she is not to send mail or appear at your home, or where you or your husband work or spend your leisure time, you are entitled to protection. Call 911 and explain your situation if you are in an emergency (say she blocks you in your driveway or says something menacing that makes you fearful for your safety). If you need protection, but are not in imminent danger, go to the local police station and file a harassment or stalking complaint against her. Once she's served with an order or summons, she should get the message that you mean business and she is to keep her distance. Unfortunately, if she is really disturbed, you might want to take extra precautions like getting an alarm system, a noisy dog, and making sure you have access to a working cell phone to call for help if you ever need it.

Alienation of Affections

If you live in Hawaii, Illinois, Mississippi, New Hampshire, New Mexico, North Carolina, South Dakota, or Utah, you might be able to sue the person who wrecked your home for money damages. These cases proceed under the theories of either alienation of affections or criminal conversation. Alienation of affections suits don't require you to prove that the homewrecker and your husband had sex. Rather, you have to show that you had a loving marriage (even if you were separated at the time), that the paramour interfered with your relationship, and that you suffered a loss or diminution of that relationship. You can prove her actions through e-mails, letters, phone records, or any other evidence showing that she made an effort to entice your mate away from you. To read a real recent alienation-of-affections case, go online to *www.aoc.state.nc.us/www/public/sc/opinions/2006/308-05-1.htm*.

Criminal conversation, on the other hand, requires proof of intercourse. If she's pregnant with, or has, your husband's child,

Nomen-clature of Divorce   Any paramour named in the adultery count of a divorce complaint (or "petition") is called a "co-respondent." That same paramour becomes the defendant (or "respondent") if you sue her directly in a separate alienation of affections or criminal conversation lawsuit.

that would certainly be sufficient evidence of the transgression. Admissions of sexual congress in e-mails, letters, or memos work well too. But whatever you do, don't "intercept" electronic or other communications using software that secretly monitors, records, copies, and stores computer data or other illegal means. If you do, you could be criminally prosecuted for violating state and federal laws protecting the sanctity of private communications. It's a better idea to retrieve "stored data" by copying the hard drive. But before committing to a course of action, it's always best to check in with an attorney licensed in your state. Most statutes of limitations require you to file your civil suit within one to three years after the event. And even if you file in time and win a big verdict in your case, you could ultimately lose. Unless a jury or judge finds that the paramour acted willfully and maliciously to specifically harm you (as opposed to harming your marriage), she can file for bankruptcy protection to discharge ("wipe out") your hard-won monetary award.

Your state might be in the majority that no longer allow spouses to file "heart balm" lawsuits against paramours. If so, you can consider whether the law in your jurisdiction and the facts of your marriage allow you to file your own civil suit against the home wrecker. Such a suit could be based upon her invasion of your privacy; her abuse of process or malicious prosecution (to stop her from filing inappropriate actions against you or to seek redress against her from having filed and lost a case against you); for intentional or negligent infliction of emotional distress (you were harmed by her outrageous actions, directed to you, and her wanton or malicious motives); or whatever other cause of action your attorney believes he or she can safely plead on your behalf without worrying that the suit will be dismissed with costs against you. After all, if you want the last word, you don't want to give her the last laugh.

CHAPTER 14

Keeping It Together

Having explored the nature of love, your mate, your marriage, and mate-poachers (how and why they operate, and what you can do to stop them and keep them permanently at bay), we'll close this book on a hopeful note, reviewing what makes a marriage last a lifetime. Let's review various mate-guarding, marriage-strengthening strategies that can help you assert your wifely rights and keep what is yours: your husband.

What Research Tells Us

To lead a healthy, long marriage, you begin by assessing the people involved. Mature, assertive, sociable, and flexible individuals with healthy self-esteem—who deem themselves worthy of love, capable of loving, and caring for another—are the best candidates for long-term marital love, satisfaction, and commitment. The optimist will have an easier time maintaining a marriage and its eight primary dimensions: sharing, role assumption and work division, uncertainty, assertiveness, time regulation, conflict management, undifferentiated space, and autonomy.

Recalling the Big Five traits, outlined on page 99, the more agreeable you and/or your partner are (that is, the more trusting, straightforward, altruistic, compliant, modest, and tenderminded), the better chance you have of sustaining a satisfying union that is less vulnerable to stress and misery. However, the higher your neuroticism score (that is, the more you tend toward anxiousness, angry hostility, depressiveness, self-consciousness, impulsiveness, or vulnerability), the more difficult you might find it to maintain fulfillment in a marriage. Even with feelings of anxiety and vulnerability, you may still have a good relationship employing effort to do the things that loving, long-term relationships require.

What things support a healthy, vital marriage that can withstand the passage of time and its many tests? Recognize the power of marriage as an independent entity and offer affection (tenderness and fondness, with physical properties) and positive feelings toward your mate. Maintaining a vital marriage entails effort, commitment, and intention. Consider the Couple Behavior Report, by researchers Sterling T. Shumway and Richard S. Wampler.

Their test assesses the following personal actions and interactions that support a relationship:

Salutary recognition: Appreciate your mate.

Small talk: Stay connected with each other's daily lives.

Ego-building comments: Admire your mate and tell him so.

Expanding shared memories: Be reflective and relive your joint history.

Exciting activities: Do fun, exciting things together.

Feedback: Provide emotional support and helpful advice that's tactful, truthful, and encouraging, even when there are faults to fix or paths to change.

Spouses who are good personal companions or who share similar morals, standards of behavior, religion, education, and culture fare better than less homogeneous mates. The happiest married couples agree on their relationship parameters: how much time to spend together versus how much alone; how much time to devote to the marriage versus individual pursuits; how they express anger and resolve conflict; and how much control each spouse has in the relationship over particular domains (such as money, sex, domestic chores, parenting, leisure time, in-laws relations, and work).

While opposites might initially attract, they are just as likely to repel over time. Optimistic opposites may draw from the positive qualities of each and create a strong bond, becoming less polarized, but most experts believe that the compatible couple has a more satisfying marriage. Symmetrical mates—those who share views on important issues, including what to expect from marriage—are more likely to enjoy a marriage that meets their expectations and gives them room to grow, while enjoying the sanctuary of a loving, exclusive relationship.

Making Marriage Pleasant

In the words of the happily married William Blake:

Love to faults is always blind,
Always is to joy inclined,
Lawless, winged, and unconfined,
And breaks all chains from every mind.

Blake got it right. A positive outlook can go a long way in supporting the conduct that cultivates a marriage and a mate. These behaviors include nipping negativity in the bud by using humor or kindness to turn things positive again; giving your partner the benefit of the doubt and trusting that he means you no harm; giving in to your partner when it's really important to him that you do so (picking your battles well); and knowing that you are spoken for and that tempting potential partners mean far more trouble to you than any momentary pleasure they could ever provide. Keep the rose-colored glasses on when it comes to your marriage and your partner, perceiving both to be the best around—and for which you are grateful.

Perceptions Matter

Maintaining a positive view of your husband and your marriage is healthy, but expecting them to be perfect is not. One of the primary findings on lasting marriages is that the happiest spouses had reasonable expectations for married life. Relationship beliefs are important. For instance, if you think you and your spouse were fated to be together (holding so-called "destiny" beliefs), you might be less inclined to do the work that is required to sustain a marriage, as you are subject to the erroneous thinking that it should run well automatically. On the other hand, if you believe that relationships and people change and require tending (that is, you hold "growth" beliefs), you might be more inclined to dig in and do whatever is necessary to make your marriage work.

Your relational beliefs affect your marriage, as well as your view of the bond you entered and whether you consider your

When Marriage Is Not the Problem	No marriage, whether covenant- or contract-based, can provide what you lack inside. If you are suffering from low self-esteem, depression, a personality disorder, or addiction, marriage itself will not improve your situation. Instead, you must address whatever individual issues you have that could be holding you back.

union a covenant or a contract. Covenantal spouses mix love with responsibility and give unselfishly of themselves to promote their union. They are, however, in danger of remaining in a marriage that is fatally flawed either by abuse, addiction, or their spouse's chronic bad behavior. Contractual spouses generally expect to get what they can from the relationship to attain self-expanding communion with their mates and individual transcendence through the experience of marriage. In a purely contractual marriage, however, when one mate is unhappy, he will be almost certain to question his commitment to a relationship that no longer satisfies him. Finally, other research reveals there are five virtues—humility, wisdom, faithfulness, industry, and self-control—that enhance the growth and depth of a satisfying, strong, enduring relationship. Who could argue with those?

Complexities of Marriage

Aside from the perception of your bond, the kind of marriage you have will affect how you relate and expect to receive or give to each other. Marriages have been categorized differently according to who classifies them. For instance, Mary Anne Fitzpatrick of the University of Washington sorted marriages into three basic groups: traditional (i.e., conventional, nonautonomous—with lots of togetherness and interdependence—and conflict avoiding); independent (i.e., nonconventional—roles are not strictly defined—semiautonomous, and engaged in active, sometimes highly expressive, conflict management); and separate (i.e., conventional in gender roles, but highly autonomous—with spouses leading basically parallel lives—and completely disengaged from conflict).

Meanwhile, Marin County psychologist, Judith Wallerstein, studied fifty happily married couples and wrote about them in *The Good Marriage: How and Why Love Lasts*. She found four marriage styles: romantic (still glowing with the memories of their blazing courtship); rescuing (where the spouses meet each other's need for help and healing from past traumas, i.e., abuse, abandonment, illness, addiction, or neglect); companionate (high in responsibility—usually both spouses work, esteem, and bound by children); or traditional (conventional gender roles, i.e., male provider, female caretaker).

I find each marriage is complex and as unique as the individuals involved. After thirty-five years in a marriage-and-family-therapy practice, I agree with Francine Klagsbrun, author of *Married People: Staying Together in the Age of Divorce*, that there are distinct characteristics found in happy, long-term marriages.

Willingness to Accommodate Change

Change will happen over time to people, cultures, and institutions; the happiest couples welcome change, viewing it as a means to grow, learn, and cope.

Adapting to What Is

Realizing that no one is perfect and that people have habits or mannerisms that will persist, the happiest couples agree to resolve what they can, and let the rest be. They handle conflicts with tact and accept what cannot be resolved with grace, humor, and loving acceptance.

Commitment to Marriage

The happiest couples share a belief that their marriage is permanent, sanctified, and a lasting bond. They know over the years that contributions might be unequal but that, over time, it evens out, and that the marriage is worthy of their efforts.

Trust Spouse

Trust is a fundamental element of a happy marriage for emotional and physical intimacy. Each spouse should feel protected, loved, and cherished by the other within the trusting refuge of the marriage.

Interdependence with Equitable Distribution of Power

The happiest couples rely on each other for support, guidance, and encouragement. They are strong autonomous individuals capable of allowing task-appropriate responsibilities to be assumed by their mate. Sensing the availability of their spouse's support and their ability to be supportive strengthens the marriage, trumping out all others.

Delighting in the Partner's Company

The happiest couples enjoy being together. They enjoy walking, talking, and other shared activities. They achieve a balance of separateness and togetherness that keep them interested in each other's individual views, pursuits, and values.

Treasuring the Well of Common Experiences

These couples cherish the life they created, with the many memories of having together weathered life's inevitable ups and downs.

Good Fortune

The happiest couples feel blessed, beginning with how they met each other to having been spared suffering during their marriage. More than anything, these couples feel fortunate to be married to their mates and are very positive in their overall outlooks on their lives and their marriages.

In addition to these eight factors, a willingness to give more than you receive and to share humor and good fun will often lead to a happy, long-term, married life. Of course, many of these aspects describe a friendship, the next topic covered on the following pages.

Physical and Emotional Friends for Life

Aristotle defined friendship as a "single soul dwelling in two bodies." To remain lovers for life, you want to handle each other with care and to commit, without wavering, to the changes time visits upon us all. Adaptation, trust, love, commitment, generosity, kindness, and mutual respect are the primary ingredients in lasting marriages.

Still, if you and your husband are like the thousands of couples studied by experts over the years, you may expect a precipitous drop in marital satisfaction two years after your wedding, and again with the birth of your children. While marital satisfaction may decline with children, their arrival tends to stabilize a couple, reducing the chance of divorce. Expect another dip in happiness at marital years twelve and nineteen (or whenever your kids are reaching puberty and leaving you, respectively). After that, however, many marriages improve—drastically. Once the burdens of childrearing and midlife are over, married lovers can reignite that dopamine flame and feel the fire of desire burning passionately once more. (You won't know till you try it.)

Holding On to What You Have

Several years ago, Linda Waite and Maggie Gallagher wrote a book called *The Case for Marriage: Why Married People Are Happier, Healthier, and Better off Financially*. In addition to being an emotional sanctuary, they claim that lasting marriage has beneficial health and financial effects, helping spouses weather common diseases and conditions such as high blood pressure, psychiatric disorders, heart disease, alcoholism, addictions, accidents, stomach disorders, cancers, and diabetes far better. Spouses tend to have healthier lifestyles and care for each other in illness. Now that you know what your marriage can do for you and what you can do for your marriage, guard both as though your life and happiness depend on them.

The Loving List

Passion and infatuation often occur without plan or intent. True love, on the other hand, with satisfaction, commitment, and complete communion, is something you can only achieve with mutual effort. Self-esteem and love expert Dr. Nathaniel Branden has a list of helpful hints to keep your love alive and your mate interested in only you:

- Verbally express your love.
- Physically (nonverbally) express your love by means of hugging, kissing, hand holding, and touching.
- Express love sexually (have sexual intimacy along with the emotions associated with it).
- Express appreciation and admiration of each other and life.
- Engage in mutual self-disclosure to a greater extent than with other people; that is, reveal yourself to your mate while maintaining high boundaries around your relationship.
- Create an emotional support system by being helpful and nurturing, respecting the other's opinions, and showing interest in the other's activities.
- Express love materially by the giving of gifts or the performance of chores.
- Accept demands from and tolerate shortcomings of the partner. (Use humor, grace, compromise, and common sense.)
- Create time to be alone together.

With knowledge and effort, you can, with your mate, transcend the bad—would-be intruders and mate-poachers, included—and embrace the beautiful and the best in your union.

The Love Scale

The following statements describe how you feel about your mate and how compatible you are in your relationship. For example, rate your answers to questions such as "Do you like your mate as a person?" on a scale from 0 to 10, depending on how strongly you feel.

0: You have no feelings at all.
5: You have a moderate feeling.
10: You have very strong feelings.

_____ 1. You take your mate's suggestions seriously.
_____ 2. You feel privileged to know your mate.
_____ 3. You feel your mate copes well with his own problems.
_____ 4. You feel your mate has unusual competence or skills.

The Love Scale, from Pam, A., R. Plutchik, and H. Conte. "Love: A Psychometric Approach," *Psychological Reports*, Vol. 37, no. 1, 1975, pp. 83–88. Reprinted with permission. Copyright 1975.

_____ 5. You feel your mate has better judgment than the average person.

_____ 6. You feel your mate is more ethical than the average person.

_____ 7. You feel your mate is more intelligent than the average person.

_____ 8. You respect your mate.

_____ 9. You and your mate can work out your difference of opinions.

_____ 10. You and your mate get along well as a couple.

_____ 11. You like sharing your experiences with your mate.

_____ 12. Your mate does not say things in public to embarrass you.

_____ 13. Your mate can accept you as you really are without change.

_____ 14. At times you seem to know exactly what your mate is thinking.

_____ 15. You are confident that your mate will stand by your side through difficult times.

_____ 16. You feel your mate understands you.

_____ 17. You are willing to make sacrifices for your mate.

_____ 18. You enjoy taking care of your mate.

_____ 19. You like going out of your way to do the things your mate enjoys.

_____ 20. You like giving your mate gifts with nothing in return.

_____ 21. You are willing to suffer for your mate to prevent your mate from suffering.

_____ 22. You do suffer when your mate is suffering.

_____ 23. You would get very angry if someone was to hurt your mate.

_____ 24. You would die for your mate.

_____ 25. It is necessary for your mate to fulfill your needs.

_____ 26. You feel it is necessary to attend all social events with your mate.

_____ 27. It is necessary for your mate to make your present personal happiness.

_____ 28. You feel good when your mate is sensitive to your moods and feelings.

_____ 29. It is important that your mate notices you.

_____ 30. You only feel secure when you are with your mate.

_____ 31. It is important that your mate praises you.

_____ 32. You would be jealous if your mate was to become involved with someone else.

_____ 33. You like being touched by your mate.

_____ 34. You always want to embrace your mate.

_____ 35. When your mate enters the room, you are sexually excited and can't wait to express that feeling.

_____ 36. You spontaneously want to express affection toward your mate when your mate is in your presence.

_____ 37. You feel your mate is better looking than the average person.

_____ 38. You like to show your mate off wherever you go.

_____ 39. Your mate is sexually attractive to you.

_____ 40. You enjoy caressing your mate.

There are (five) subscales to this questionnaire. They are:

1. Respect
2. Congeniality
3. Altruism
4. Attachment
5. Physical attraction

To find your score on each subscale, add the items belonging to each subscale as follows:

Respect: Questions 1–8
Congeniality: Questions 9–16
Altruism: Questions 17–24
Attachment: Questions 25–32
Physical Attraction: Questions 33–40

Higher scores indicate higher levels of characteristics per each section above. Check your compatibility with your mate. Then compare with your mate for likeness.

Ego Defense Mechanisms

Aggression: Acting out in a hostile, unacceptable way that polite society would not accept.

Avoidance: The act of removing oneself from another.

Compartmentalization: The act of separating parts of self from awareness of other parts and acting with separate sets of values. For instance, a man cheats on his wife, yet is a leader of a couples' support group.

Compensation: This mechanism is manifested when a person compensates or makes up for something with other behavior. Let's say you do not meet your partner's physical needs; you buy him expensive watches or suits to make up for your disinterest in sex.

Counter transference: The feelings attributed by the therapist towards the patient. The therapist must be aware of this issue while treating patients.

Denial: A mechanism that allows us to refuse to accept the reality of a situation. It is the major mechanism used by substance abusers, alcoholics, gamblers, and pedophiles. If your partner is a sex addict, he might say that he only sleeps with other women occasionally and can stop any time he wants to. The truth is, he cannot stop without help. Don't confuse denial with lying. Lying is conscious behavior, while denial is unconscious.

Displacement: This mechanism focuses on another person or object, the anger or other negative feelings which cannot be dealt with toward the appropriate person or object due to fear of recrimination.

Emotional insulation: Withdrawal in some form to protect oneself from hurt. For instance, a person who claims to be shy may be using this mechanism to avoid socializing.

Fantasy: This mechanism is our mind's way of taking us to a more pleasurable place, to give us freedom from an uncomfortable situation.

Humor: This mechanism fools many people because in general, we consider humor to be happy, light, and fun, but much humor is based on making fun at someone's expense. If the "humor" is not funny, it's mocking and derisive and generally masks anger or hostility.

Idealization: This is when you give someone or something greater value than it deserves, like placing someone on the proverbial pedestal.

Identification: We all use this mechanism at some time in our lives. It starts out when we are babies and we identify with our mother (or caregiver) and her smile or her look. Then we identify with our father and other people in our environment. This identification process occurs throughout our growth and development. By identification, we take on inner emotional qualities, as well as some imitated outer characteristics. We acquire the good and the bad qualities of those with whom we identify.

Introjection: With this mechanism we take on the qualities, wants, likes, or dislikes of another who is emotionally important to us.

Passive aggression: This mechanism allows people to hurt or offend or obstruct us, yet we are not really sure if what they said or did was intentional or not.

Projection: This refers to the unconscious process whereby we place or cast our own objectionable or unacceptable thought on another.

Rationalization: This mechanism allows us to salvage our ego when we are in pain. We come up with an unconscious, plausible reason for relief from the anguish we may be feeling.

Reaction formation: This is when you unconsciously do the opposite behavior from that with which you identified.

Regression: This mechanism is when a person goes back to a former stage of development where he was more content and secure.

Repression: This mechanism protects us from situations that we find emotionally intolerable and typically so hurtful that we cannot bring forth the situation to consciousness without the help of some form of analysis.

Somatization: The mind's unconscious conversion of emotional distress into physical distress.

Sublimation: This is when a person makes something that is socially unacceptable into something which is acceptable to mainstream society.

Suppression: The mechanism that allows us to put hurtful situations or feelings out of our everyday thoughts. This is usually less painful material than the matters we repress, which we cannot even begin to deal with unless somehow released from our unconscious. Suppressed material can be brought forth without therapy. (It's still best to have a mental health-care professional guide you through the process of dealing with suppressed material.)

Transference: The feelings we attribute to the therapist, who may come to represent various people in your life (parents, wife, teacher, abuser, siblings, relatives, and the like) at different times during the therapeutic process. In this way, transference allows a person to work out issues (and the people involved) in an emotionally safe, nonthreatening, professionally directed environment, hopefully resolving them while in treatment.

Undoing: The method we use to try to make things right which we feel we have done wrong. If your partner has had an affair, he may come home with tickets for that opera you've been bugging him to see with you. The idea of undoing is that it will supersede the person's "bad" behavior.

Withdrawal: The process by which a person removes himself—either physically or emotionally—from a situation that he finds unacceptable. Withdrawal provides a temporary fix at best, merely postponing the inevitable situation that must be addressed.

Sexual Self-Efficacy Scale for Female Functioning

The form on the following pages lists sexual activities that women engage in.

For women respondents only: Under Column I (Can Do), check the activities you think you could do if you were asked to do them today. For only those activities you checked in Column I, rate your degree of confidence that you could do them by selecting a number from 10 to 100 using the scale given below. Write this number in Column II (Confidence).

For male partners only: Under Column I (Can Do), check the activities you think your female partner could do if she were

Sexual Self-Efficacy Scale for Female Functioning (SSES-F), from Bailes, S., L. Creti, C.S. Fichten, E. Libman, W. Brender, and R. Amsel, "Sexual Self-Efficacy Scale for Female Functioning (SSES-F)," in C.M. Davis, W.L. Yarber, R. Bauserman, G. Schreer, and S.L. Davis (eds.), *Handbook of Sexuality-Related Measures* (pp. 531–534). (Thousand Oaks, California: Sage Publications, 1998). Copyright 1998, Bailes, S., L. Creti, C.S. Fichten, E. Libman, W. Brender, and R. Amsel. Reprinted by permission of Sage Publications, Inc.

asked to do them today. For only those activities you checked in Column I, rate your degree of confidence that your female partner could do them by selecting a number from 10 to 100, with 10 being Quite Uncertain, 50–60 being Moderately Certain, and 100 being Quite Certain. Write this number in Column II (Confidence). If you think your partner is not able to do a particular activity, leave Columns I and II blank for that activity.

Activity	Check if female can do	Rate confidence 10 to 100
Anticipate (think about) having intercourse without fear or anxiety.		
Feel comfortable being nude with the partner.		
Feel comfortable with your body.		
In general, feel good about your ability to respond sexually.		
Be interested in sex.		
Feel sexual desire for the partner.		
Feel sexually desirable to the partner.		
Initiate an exchange of affection without feeling obliged to have sexual relations.		
Initiate sexual activities.		
Refuse a sexual advance by the partner.		
Cope with the partner's refusal of your sexual advance.		
Ask the partner to provide the type and amount of sexual stimulation needed.		
Provide the partner with the type and amount of sexual stimulation requested.		

Activity	Check if female can do	Rate confidence 10 to 100
Deal with discrepancies in sexual preference between you and your partner.		
Enjoy an exchange of affection without having sexual relations.		
Enjoy a sexual encounter with a partner without having intercourse.		
Enjoy having your body caressed by the partner (excluding genitals and breasts).		
Enjoy having your genitals caressed by the partner.		
Enjoy having your breasts caressed by the partner.		
Enjoy caressing the partner's body (excluding genitals).		
Enjoy caressing the partner's genitals.		
Enjoy intercourse.		
Enjoy a lovemaking encounter in which you do not reach orgasm.		
Feel sexually aroused in response to erotica (pictures, books, films, etc.).		
Become sexually aroused by masturbating when alone.		
Become sexually aroused during foreplay when both partners are clothed.		
Become sexually aroused during foreplay when both partners are nude.		
Maintain sexual arousal throughout a sexual encounter.		
Become sufficiently lubricated to engage in intercourse.		

Activity	Check if female can do	Rate confidence 10 to 100
Engage in intercourse without pain or discomfort.		
Have an orgasm while masturbating when alone.		
Have an orgasm while the partner stimulates you by means other than intercourse.		
Have an orgasm during intercourse with concurrent stimulation of the clitoris.		
Have an orgasm during intercourse without concurrent stimulation of the clitoris.		
Stimulate a partner to orgasm by means other than intercourse.		
Stimulate a partner to orgasm by means of intercourse.		
Reach orgasm within a reasonable period of time.		

Mate Retention Inventory

Please write in the blank to the left of each item the number that best represents how frequently you performed the act within the past ONE year. For example, if you never performed the act within the past one year, write a "0" in the blank to the left of the item. Not all questions from the original pertain to married individuals, and some have been revised to be inclusive of unmarried people. There is no scoring system, as the inventory is designed for you to recognize behaviors you've done that you may not have noticed before.

_____ 1. Called at unexpected times to see whom my partner was with.

_____ 2. Did not take my partner to a party where other women would be present.

_____ 3. Flirted with someone in front of my partner.

_____ 4. Spent all my free time with my partner so that he could not meet anyone else.

From Shackelford, Goetz, and Buss, "Mate Retention In Marriage: Further Evidence of the Reliability of the Mate Retention Inventory," *Personality and Individual Differences* 39 (2005): 415–25. Copyright © 2005. Reprinted with permission of Elsevier.

_____ 5. Became angry when my partner flirted too much.

_____ 6. Cried when my partner said he might go out with someone else.

_____ 7. Told my partner I wanted to remain married.

_____ 8. Cut down the appearance of other women.

_____ 9. Spent a lot of money on my partner.

_____ 10. Gave in to my partner's sexual requests.

_____ 11. Dressed nicely to maintain my partner's interest.

_____ 12. Told my partner "I love you."

_____ 13. Told my partner that I would change in order to please him.

_____ 14. Introduced my partner as my spouse or romantic partner.

_____ 15. Held my partner's hand when other women were around.

_____ 16. Asked my partner to wear an article of clothing that I gave him (i.e., hat, tie, scarf, jacket).

_____ 17. Told other women terrible things about my partner so that they wouldn't like him.

_____ 18. Yelled at a woman who looked at my partner.

_____ 19. Hit a woman who made a pass at my partner.

_____ 20. Called to make sure my partner was where he said he would be.

_____ 21. Refused to introduce my partner to my same-sex friends.

_____ 22. Insisted that my partner stay at home rather than going out.

_____ 23. Picked a fight with a woman who was interested in my partner.

_____ 24. Made my partner feel guilty about talking to another woman.

_____ 25. Made up my face to look nice.

_____ 26. Got pregnant so my partner would stay with me.

_____ 27. Started a bad rumor about another woman.

_____ 28. Bought my partner an expensive gift.

_____ 29. Acted sexy to take my partner's mind off other women.

_____ 30. Wore the latest fashion to enhance my appearance.

_____ 31. Went out of my way to be kind, nice, and caring.

_____ 32. Told my same-sex friends how much my partner and I were in love.

_____ 33. Kissed my partner when other women were around.

_____ 34. Asked my partner to wear his ring.

_____ 35. Told other women that my partner was not a nice person.

_____ 36. Stared coldly at a woman who was looking at my partner.

_____ 37. Became a "slave" to my partner.

_____ 38. Ignored my partner when he started flirting with others.

_____ 39. Had my friends check up on my partner.

_____ 40. Went out with another man to make my partner jealous.

_____ 41. Bought my partner flowers.

_____ 42. Diminished the attractiveness of another woman.

_____ 43. Took my partner away from a gathering where other women were around.

_____ 44. Threatened a woman who was making moves on my partner.

_____ 45. Gave my partner jewelry to signify that he was taken.

_____ 46. Told other women that my partner was stupid.

_____ 47. Monopolized my partner's time at a social gathering.

_____ 48. Threatened to break up if my partner ever cheated on me.

_____ 49. Bragged about my partner to other women.

_____ 50. Gave in to my partner's every wish.

_____ 51. Got my friends to beat up someone who was interested in my partner.

_____ 52. Held my partner closer when another woman walked into the room.

_____ 53. Snooped through my partner's personal belongings.

_____ 54. Pointed out to my partner the flaws of another woman.

_____ 55. Performed sexual favors to keep my partner around.

_____ 56. Wore my partner's clothes in front of others.

_____ 57. Told other women that my partner might have a sexually transmitted disease.

_____ 58. Complimented my partner on his appearance.

_____ 59. Questioned my partner about what he did when we were apart.

_____ 60. Told my partner that we needed a total commitment to each other.

_____ 61. Took my partner out to a nice restaurant.

_____ 62. Mentioned to other women that my partner was taken.

_____ 63. Told my partner that the other person he is interested in has slept with nearly everyone.

_____ 64. Dropped by unexpectedly to see what my partner was doing.

_____ 65. Yelled at my partner after he showed interest in another woman.

_____ 66. Told my partner that I was dependent on my partner.

_____ 67. Made sure that I looked nice for my partner.

_____ 68. Gave a woman a dirty look when she looked at my partner.

_____ 69. Pretended to be mad so that my partner would feel guilty.

_____ 70. At a party, did not let my partner out of my sight.

_____ 71. Hit my partner when I caught him flirting with someone else.

_____ 72. Went along with everything my partner said.

_____ 73. Told other women to stay away from my partner.

_____ 74. Bought my partner some jewelry (for example, ring, watch, neck chain).

_____ 75. Told my partner I would "die" if he ever left me.

_____ 76. Read my partner's personal mail.

_____ 77. Insisted that my partner spend all his free time with me.

_____ 78. Cried in order to keep my partner with me.

_____ 79. Told my partner that another woman was stupid.

_____ 80. Was helpful when my partner really needed it.

_____ 81. Vandalized the property of a woman who made a pass at my partner.

_____ 82. Said that I would never talk to my partner again if I saw him with someone else.

_____ 83. Have sex with my partner to deepen our bond.

_____ 84. Put my arm around my partner in front of others.

_____ 85. Threatened to harm myself if my partner ever left me.

_____ 86. Displayed greater affection for my partner.

_____ 87. Confronted someone who had made a pass at my partner.

_____ 88. Told others the intimate things we had done together.

_____ 89. Stayed close to my partner while we were at a party.

_____ 90. Talked to another man at a party to make my partner jealous.

_____ 91. Bought my partner a small gift.

_____ 92. Told others my partner was a pain.

_____ 93. Sat next to my partner when others were around.

_____ 94. Made myself "extra attractive" for my partner.

_____ 95. Told my partner that another woman was out to use him.

_____ 96. Did not let my partner talk to other women.

_____ 97. Gave in to sexual pressure to keep my partner.

_____ 98. Hung up a picture of my partner so others would know he was taken.

_____ 99. Became jealous when my partner went out without me.

_____ 100. Slapped a woman who made a pass at my partner.

_____ 101. Pleaded that I could not live without my partner.

_____ 102. Would not let my partner go out without me.

_____ 103. Acted against my will to let my partner have his way.

_____ 104. Showed interest in another man to make my partner angry.

References

Chapter 1 References

Feeney, J. A., P. Noller, and V. J. Callan. "Attachment Style, Communication and Satisfaction in the Early Years of Marriage," *Advances in Personal Relationships*, Vol. 5, 1994, pp. 269–308.

Fowers, B. J., K. H. Montel, and D. H. Olson. "Predicting Marital Success Based on Couple Types," *Journal of Marital & Family Therapy*, Vol. 22, no. 1, 1996, pp. 103–11.

Gottman, John M., with Silver, Nan. *Why Marriages Succeed or Fail . . . And How You Can Make Yours Last* (New York, NY: Simon & Schuster, 1994).

Gottman, John M., Silver, Nan. *The Seven Principles for Making Marriage Work* (New York, NY: Crown, 2000).

Hazan, C., and P.R. Shaver. "Romantic Love Conceptualized As an Attachment Process," *Journal of Personality and Social Psychology*, Vol. 52, 1987, pp. 512–24.

Hazan, C., and P.R. Shaver. "Attachment As an Organizational Framework for Research on Close Relationships," *Psychological Enquiry*, Vol. 5, no. l, 1994, pp. 1–22.

Heiman, J.R., and C.M. Meston. "Empirically Validated Treatment for Sexual Dysfunction," *Annual Review of Sex Research*, Vol. 8, 1997, pp. 148–94.

Kunce, L. J., and P. R. Shaver. "An Attachment-Theoretical Approach to Caregiving in Romantic Relationships," in K. Bartholomew, and D. Perlman (eds.), *Advances in Personal Relationships*, Vol. 5 (London, UK: Jessica Kingsley Publishers, 1994).

Maslow, A. H. "A Theory of Human Motivation," *Psychological Review*, Vol. 50, 1943, pp. 370–96.

Maslow, A. H. *Motivation and Personality* (New York, NY: Harper, 1954).

Maslow, A. H. *The Farther Reaches of Human Nature* (New York, NY: The Viking Press, 1971).

Mikulincer, M., V. Florian, P.A. Cowan, and C.P. Cowan. "Attachment Security in Couple Relationships: A Systemic Model and Its Implications for Family Dynamics," *Family Process*, Vol. 41. no. 3, 2002, pp. 405–34.

Schaefer, M. T., and D. H. Olson. "Assessing Intimacy: The PAIR Inventory," *Journal of Marital and Family Therapy*, Vol. 7, 1981, pp. 47–60.

Shaver, P., C. Hazan, and D. Bradshaw. "Love As Attachment: The Integration of Three Behavioural Systems." In R. J. Sternberg, and M. Barnes (eds.), *Anatomy of Love* (New Haven, CT: Yale University Press, 1988).

Waring, E. M., D. McElrath, D. Lefcoe, and G. Weisz. "Dimensions of Intimacy in Marriage," *Psychiatry*, Vol. 44, 1981, pp. 169–75.

Waring, E. M., and J. R. Reddon. "The Measurement of Intimacy in Marriage: The Waring Intimacy Questionnaire," *Journal of Clinical Psychology*, Vol. 39, no. 1, 1983, pp. 53–7.

Chapter 2 References

Acitelli, L. K. "Maintaining and Enhancing a Relationship by Attending to It." In J. Harvey and A. Wenzel (eds.), *Close Romantic Relationships:*

Maintenance and Enhancement (Mahwah, NJ: Lawrence Erlbaum Associates, Inc., 2001).

Amato, P. R., and A. Booth. "A Prospective Study of Divorce and Parent–Child Relationships," *Journal of Marriage and the Family*, Vol. 58, 1996, pp. 356–65.

Browne, Marie H., with Marlene Browne. *If the Man You Love Was Abused* (Avon, MA: Adams Media, 2007).

Buss, D. M., R. J. Larsen, and D. Westen. "Sex Differences in Jealousy: Not Gone, Not Forgotten, and Not Explained By Alternative Hypotheses," *Psychological Science*, Vol. 7, 1996, pp. 373–75.

Buss, D. M., and T. K. Shackelford. "From Vigilance to Violence: Mate Retention Tactics in Married Couples," *Journal of Personality and Social Psychology*, Vol. 72, 1997, pp. 346–61.

Buss, D. M., T. K. Shackelford, L. A. Kirkpatrick, J. C. Choe, H. K. Lim, M. Hasegawa, T. Hasegawa, and K. Bennett. "Jealousy and the Nature of Beliefs About Infidelity: Tests of Competing Hypotheses About Sex Differences in the United States, Korea, and Japan," *Personal Relationships*, Vol. 6, 1999, pp. 125–50.

Caughlin, J. P. "The Demand/Withdraw Pattern of Communication as a Predictor of Marital Satisfaction over Time: Unresolved Issues and Future Directions," *Human Communication Research*, Vol. 28, 2002, pp. 49–86.

Cobb, R.J., J. Davila, and T.N. Bradbury. "Attachment Security and Marital Satisfaction: The Role of Positive Perceptions and Social Support," *Personality and Social Psychology Bulletin*, Vol. 27, 2001, pp. 1131–43.

Dainton, M. "Maintenance Behaviors, Expectations For Maintenance, and Satisfaction: Linking Comparison Levels To Relational Maintenance Strategies," *Journal of Social and Personal Relationships*, Vol. 17, 2000, pp. 827–42.

Dutton, D. G., and D. Sonkin. "Treating Assaultive Men from an Attachment Perspective," in D. G. Dutton, and D. Sonkin (eds.), *Intimate Violence: Contemporary Treatment Innovations* (New York: Haworth Maltreatment & Trauma Press, 2003).

Heene, Els L.D., A. Buysse, and P. Oost. "Indirect Pathways Between Depressive Symptoms and Marital Distress: The Role of Conflict Communication, Attributions, and Attachment Style," *Family Process*, Vol. 44, no. 4, 2005, pp. 413–40.

O'Farrell, K. J., E. B. Rosenthal, and E.C. O'Neal. "Relationship Satisfaction and Responsiveness to Nonmates' Flirtation: An Evolutionary Explanation," *Journal of Social and Personal Relationships*, Vol. 20, 2003, pp. 663–74.

Parke, R. D. "Fathers and Families," in M. H. Bornstein (ed.), *Handbook of Parenting Volume 3* (Mahwah, NJ: Lawrence Erlbaum Associates, Inc., 1995).

Rusbult, C. E., D. J. Johnson, and G. D. Morrow. "Predicting Satisfaction and Commitment in Adult Romantic Involvements: An Assessment of the Generalizability of the Investment Model," *Social Psychology Quarterly*, Vol. 49, 1986, pp. 81–9.

Schmitt, D.P., and D.M. Buss. "Human Mate Poaching: Tactics and Temptations For Infiltrating Existing Relationships," *Journal of Personality and Social Psychology*, Vol. 80, 2001, pp. 894–917.

Shackelford, T. K., and D. M. Buss. "Cues to Infidelity," *Personality and Social Psychology Bulletin*, Vol. 23, 1997, pp. 1034–45.

Shackelford, T. K., D. M. Buss, and K. Bennett. "Forgiveness or Breakup: Sex Differences in Responses to a Partner's Infidelity," *Cognition and Emotion*, Vol. 16, 2002, pp. 299–307.

Frankl, Victor, E. *Man's Search for Meaning: An Introduction to Logotherapy* (New York: Washington Square Press, 1963).

Chapter 3 References

For the duty to disclose and protect spouses from HIV and other STDs, see recent (3 July 2006) Supreme Court of California case: *John B. v. The Superior Court of Los Angeles County*, No. S128248, at *www.courtinfo.ca.gov/opinions/documents/S128248.PDF*.

Bleske, A. L., and D. M. Buss. "Can Men and Women Be Just Friends?" *Personal Relationships*, Vol. 21, 2000, pp. 131–51.

Bleske, A. L., and T. K. Shackelford. "Poaching, Promiscuity, and Deceit: Combating Mating Rivalry in Same-Sex Friendships," *Personal Relationships*, Vol. 8, 2001, pp. 407–24.

Bleske-Rechek, A. L., and D. M. Buss. "Opposite-Sex Friendship: Sex Differences and Similarities in Initiation, Selection, and Dissolution," *Personality and Social Psychology Bulletin*, Vol. 27, 2001, pp. 1310–23.

Buxton, Amity Pierce. *The Other Side of the Closet: The Coming-Out Crisis for Straight Spouses and Families* (New York: John Wiley & Sons, Inc., 1994).

Festinger, L., S. Schachter, and K.W. Back. *Social Pressures in Informal Groups: A Study of Human Factors in Housing* (New York: Harper & Bros., 1950).

Fisher, Helen. *Anatomy of Love: A Natural History of Monogamy, Adultery and Divorce* (New York: Simon & Schuster, 1992).

Gochros, Jean Schaar. *When Husbands Come Out of the Closet* (New York: Haworth Press, 1989).

Major, B., P.I. Carrington, and P.J. Carnevale. "Physical Attractiveness and Self-Esteem: Attributions for Praise from Other-Sex Evaluator." *Personality and Social Psychology Bulletin*, Vol. 10, 1984, pp. 43–50.

Quan, Tracy. "The End of Girltalk?" *Salon.com*, 4 February 1998.

Richardson, Laurel. *The New Other Woman: Contemporary Single Women in Affairs with Married Men* (New York: The Free Press, 1985).

Richardson, L. "Secrecy and Status: The Social Construction of Forbidden Relationships," *American Sociological Review*, Vol. 53, 1988, pp. 209–19.

Rotello, Gabriel. "Malcolm Forbes Outed March 1990: A Cover Story in Outweek Edited by Gabriel Rotello, Launches the Outing Debate—Changing Perceptions," *The Advocate*, 12 Nov 2002.

Shackelford, T. K., and D. M. Buss. "Cues to Infidelity," *Personality and Social Psychology Bulletin*, Vol. 23, 1997, pp. 1034–45.

Schmitt, D.P., and D.M. Buss. "Human Mate Poaching: Tactics and Temptations for Infiltrating Existing Relationships," *Journal of Personality and Social Psychology*, Vol. 80, 2001, pp. 894–917.

Shackelford, T. K., D. M. Buss, and K. Bennett. "Forgiveness or Breakup: Sex Differences in Responses to a Partner's Infidelity," *Cognition and Emotion*, Vol. 16, 2002, pp. 299–307.

Sprecher, S., P.C. Regan, and K. McKinney. "Beliefs About the Outcomes of Extramarital Sexual Relationships As a Function of the Gender of the 'Cheating Spouse.'" *Sex Roles: A Journal of Research*, Vol. 38, nos. 3–4, 1998, pp. 301–11.

Tuch, Richard. *The Single Woman-Married Man Syndrome: Masochism, Ambivalence, Splitting, Vulnerability, and Self-Deception* (Northvale, NJ: Jason Aronson Inc., 2000).

Tuch, Richard. "The Single Woman-Married Man Syndrome," *Journal of the American Medical Association*, Vol. 285, no. 19, 2001, pp. 2513–14.

Vincent, Norah. *Self-Made Man: One Woman's Journey into Manhood and Back* (New York: Viking, 2006).

Viorst, Judith. *Necessary Losses* (New York: Simon & Schuster, 1986).

Wilson, Glenn. *The Great Sex Divide* (England: Peter Owen Publishers, 1989).

Chapter 4 References

American Psychiatric Association (2000). *Diagnostic and Statistical Manual of Mental Disorders*: Fourth Edition, Text Revision. Washington, D.C.: American Psychiatric Association.

Benning, S.D., C.J. Patrick, B.M. Hicks, D.M. Blonigen, and R.F. Krueger. "Factor Structure of the Psychopathic Personality Inventory: Validity and Implications for Clinical Assessment," *Psychological Assessment*, Vol. 15, no. 3, 2003, pp. 340–350.

Paris, J., and S. Braverman. "Successful and Unsuccessful Marriages in Borderline Patients," *Journal of the American Academy of Psychoanalysis*, Vol. 23, no. 1, 1995, pp. 153–66.

Yen, S., S. Zlotnick, and E. Costello. "Affect Regulation in Women with Borderline Personality Disorder Traits." *Journal of Nervous and Mental Disease*, Vol. 190, no. 10, 2002, pp. 693–96.

Chapter 5 References

Anderson, T.L. "Relationships Among Internet Attitudes, Internet Use, Romantic Beliefs, and Perceptions of Online Romantic Relationships," *Cyberpsychology & Behavior*, Vol. 8, no. 6, 2005.

Atkins, D.C., D.H. Baucom, and N.S. Jacobson. "Understanding Infidelity: Correlates in a National Random Sample," *Journal of Family Psychology*, Vol. 15, no. 4, 2001, pp. 735–49.

Atkins, D.C., J. Yi, D.H. Baucom, and A. Christensen. "Infidelity in Couples Seeking Marital Therapy," *Journal of Family Psychology*, Vol. 19, no. 3, 2005, pp. 470–73.

Aviram, I., and Y. Amichai-Hamburger. "Online Infidelity: Aspects of Dyadic Satisfaction, Self-Disclosure, and Narcissism," *Journal of Computer-Mediated Communication*, Vol. 10, no. 3, 2005, article 1.

Baumeister, R. F., and E. Bratslavsky. "Passion, Intimacy, and Time: Passionate Love as a Function of Change in Intimacy," *Personality and Social Psychology Review*, Vol. 3, 1999, pp. 49–67.

Carlson, Margaret. "Divorce, Kennedy-Style: A New Book and Another Scandal May Finally Hit the Kennedys Where it Would Hurt—In the Ballot Box," *Time Magazine*, 12 May 2006.

Drigotas, S. M., and W. Barta. "The Cheating Heart: Scientific Explorations of Infidelity," *Current Directions in Psychological Science*, Vol. 10, 2001, pp. 177–80.

Ling, R. "Direct and Mediated Interaction in the Maintenance of Social Relationships," in Sloane, A., and F. van Rijn (eds.) *Home Informatics and Telematics: Information, Technology and Society* (Boston, MA: Kluwer, 2000).

Olenick, I. "Odds of Spousal Infidelity Are Influenced by Social and Demographic Factors," *Family Planning Perspectives*. 2000.

Shackelford, T.K., A.T. Goetz, and D.M. Buss. "Mate Retention and Marriage: Further Evidence of the Reliability of the Mate Retention Inventory," *Personality and Individual Differences*, Vol. 39, 2005, pp. 415–426.

Træen, B., and H. Stigum. "Parallel Sexual Relationships in the Norwegian Context," *Journal of Community & Applied Social Psychology*, Vol. 8, 1998, pp. 41–56.

Treas, J., and D. Giesen. "Sexual Infidelity Among Married and Cohabiting Americans," *Journal of Marriage and the Family*, Vol. 62, 2000, pp. 48–60.

Wendi Deng Biography. *Investing Value.com*.

Chapter 6 References

Costa, P. T., Jr., and R. R. McCrae. *Revised NEO Personality Inventory (NEO-P1-K) and NEO Five-Factor Inventory (NEO-FFI) Professional Manual* (Odessa, FL: Psychological Assessment Resources, 1992).

Costa, P. T., Jr., and R. R. McCrae. "Set Like Plaster? Evidence for the Stability of Adult Personality," in T. Heatherton, and J. L. Weinberger (eds.), *Can Personality Change?* (Washington, DC: American Psychological Association, 1994).

Costa, P. T., Jr., and R. R. McCrae. "Domains and Facets: Hierarchical Personality Assessment Using the Revised NEO Personality Inventory," *Journal of Personality Assessment*, Vol. 64, 1995, pp. 21–50.

Drigotas, S. M., and W. Barta. "The Cheating Heart: Scientific Explorations of Infidelity," *Current Directions in Psychological Science*, Vol. 10, 2001, pp. 177–80.

Kelly, E.L., and J.J. Conley. "Personality and Compatibility: A Prospective Analysis of Marital Stability and Marital Satisfaction," *Journal of Personality and Social Psychology*, Vol. 52, no. 1, 1987, pp. 27–40.

Koback, R., and C. Hazan. "Attachment in Marriage: Effects of Security and Accuracy of Working Models," *Journal of Personality and Social Psychology*, Vol. 60, no. 6, 1991, pp. 861–869.

Kohut, Heinz. *The Analysis of the Self* (New York: International Universities Press, Inc., 1971).

Larson, J.H., C.H. Hammond, and J.M. Harper. "Perceived Equity and Intimacy in Marriage," *Journal of Marital and Family Therapy*, 1998.

Lusterman, D. "Repetitive Infidelity, Womanizing, and Don Juanism," in R. Levant, and G. Brooks (eds.), *Men and Sex* (New York: John Wiley & Sons, Inc., 1997).

Lynam, D.R., and T.A. Widiger. "Using the Five-Factor Model to Represent the DSM-IV Personality Disorders: An Expert Consensus Approach," *Journal of Abnormal Psychology*, Vol. 110, no. 3, 2001, pp. 401–12.

Marioles, N., D. P. Strickert, and A. L. Hammer. "Attraction, Satisfaction, and Psychological Types of Couples," *Journal of Psychological Type*, Vol. 35, 1995, pp. 10–21.

Rosenthal, R., and D. B. Rubin. "Interpersonal Expectancy Effects: The First 345 Studies," *Behavioral and Brain Sciences*, Vol. 3, 1978, pp. 377–86.

Snyder, M. "When Belief Creates Reality," in M.P. Zanna (ed.), *Advances in Experimental Social Psychology* 18 (Orlando, FL: Academic Press, 1984).

Walster, E., J. Traupmann, and G.W. Walster. "Equity and Extramarital Sexuality," *Archives of Sexual Behavior*, Vol. 7, 1978, pp. 127–42.

Watson, D., E.C. Klohnen, A. Casillas, E.N. Simms, J. Haig, and D.S. Berry. "Match Makers and Deal Breakers: Analyses of Assortative Mating in Newlywed Couples," *Journal of Personality*, Vol. 72, no. 5, 2004, pp. 1029–68.

Chapter 7 References

Bailes, S., L. Creti, C.S., Fichten, E. Libman, W. Brender, and R. Amsel. "Sexual Self-Efficacy Scale for Female Functioning (SSES-F)," in C.M. Davis, W.L. Yarber, R. Bauserman, G. Schreer, and S.L. Davis (eds.). *Handbook of Sexuality-Related Measures* (Thousand Oaks, CA: Sage Publications, 1998).

Campbell, A. *A Mind of Her Own: The Evolutionary Psychology of Women* (New York: Oxford University Press, 2002).

Christopher, F. S., and S. Sprecher. "Sexuality in Marriage, Dating, and Other Relationships: A Decade Review," *Journal of Marriage and the Family*, Vol. 62, 2000. pp. 999–1017.

Geary, D. C. *Male, Female: The Evolution of Human Sex Differences* (Washington, D.C.: American Psychological Association, 1998).

Geary, D.C., J. Vigil, J. Byrd-Craven. "Evolution of Human Mate Choice," *Journal of Sex Research*. 2004.

Grammar, K., L. Renniger, and B. Fischer. "Disco Clothing, Female Sexual Motivation, and Relationship Status: Is She Dressed to Impress?" *The Journal of Sex Research*, Vol. 41, 2004, pp. 66–74.

Gangestad, S.W., and J.A. Simpson. "On the Evolutionary Psychology of Human Mating: Trade-Offs and Strategic Pluralism," *Behavioral and Brain Sciences*, Vol. 23, 2000, pp. 573–587.

Hicks, T., and H. Leitenberg. "Sexual Fantasies About One's Partner Versus Someone Else: Gender Differences in Incidence and Frequency," *Journal of Sex Research*, Vol. 38, 2001, pp. 43–50.

Langlois, J., L. Kalakanis, A. Rubenstein, A. Larson, M. Hallam, and M. Smoot. "The Myths of Beauty: A Meta-Analytic and Theoretical Review," *Psychological Bulletin*, Vol. 126, no. 3, 2000, pp. 390–423.

Laumann, Edward O., John H. Gagnon, Robert T. Michael, and Stuart Michaels. *The Social Organization of Sexuality in the United States* (Chicago, IL: University of Chicago Press, 1994).

Lawrance, K., and E. S. Byers. "Sexual Satisfaction in Long-Term Heterosexual Relationships: The Interpersonal Exchange Model of Sexual Satisfaction," *Personal Relationships*, Vol. 2, 1995, pp. 267–85.

Michael, R.T (2003). "An Economic Perspective on Sex, Marriage and the Family in Contemporary United States," in Steven M. Tipton, and John Witte, Jr (eds.), *Family Transformed: Religion, Values, and Society in American Life* (Washington, DC: Georgetown University Press, 2005).

Olson, I.R., and C. Marshuetz. "Facial Attractiveness Is Appraised in a Glance," *Emotion*, Vol. 5, no. 4, 2005, pp. 498–502.

Rusbult, C. E., J. J. Martz, and C. R. Agnew. "The Investment Model Scale: Measuring Commitment Level, Satisfaction Level, Quality of Alternatives, and Investment Size," *Personal Relationships*, Vol. 5, 1998, pp. 357–91.

Wegner, D. M., T. Giuliano, and P. Hertel. "Cognitive Interdependence in Close Relationships," in W. J. Ickes (ed.), *Compatible and Incompatible Relationships* (New York, NY: Springer-Verlag, 1985).

Chapter 8 References

Allen, E.S., and D.C. Atkins. "The Multidimensional and Developmental Nature of Infidelity: A Clinical Framework," *In Session: Psychotherapy in Practice*, Vol. 61, 2005, pp. 1371–1382.

Allen, E. S., and D. H. Baucom. "Adult Attachment and Patterns of Extradyadic Involvement," *Family Process*, Vol. 43, 2004, pp. 467–488.

Atkins, D.C., K.E. Eldridge, D.H. Baucom, and A. Christensen. "Behavioral Marital Therapy and Infidelity: Optimism in the Face of Betrayal," *Journal of Consulting and Clinical Psychology*, Vol. 73, 2005, pp. 144–50.

Atkins, D.C., J. Yi, D.H. Baucom, A. Christensen. "Infidelity in Couples Seeking Marital Therapy," *Journal of Family Psychology*, Vol. 19, no. 3, 2005, pp. 470–3.

Atwood, J.D., and M. Seifer. "Extramarital Affairs and Constructed Meanings: A Social Constructionist Therapeutic Approach," *American Journal of Family Therapy*, Vol. 25, 1997, pp. 55–74.

Bozon, M (2001). "Sexuality, Gender, and the Couple: A Sociohistorical Perspective," *Annual Review of Sex Research*.

Bray, J.H., and E.N. Jouriles. "Treatment of Marital Conflict and Prevention of Divorce," *Journal of Marital and Family Therapy*, Vol. 21, 1995, pp. 461–73.

Brown, Emily M. *Patterns of Infidelity and Their Treatment* (New York: Brunner/Mazel, 1991).

Doss, B.D., D.C. Atkins, and A. Christensen. "Who's Dragging Their Feet? Husbands and Wives Seeking Marital Therapy," *Journal of Marital and Family Therapy*, Vol. 29, no. 2, 2003, pp. 165–77.

Drigotas, S., and W. Barta. "The Cheating Heart: Scientific Explorations of Infidelity." *Current Directions in Psychological Science*, Vol. 20, no. 5, 2001, pp. 177–80.

Gordon, K.C., and D.H. Baucom. "A Multitheoretical Intervention for Promoting Recovery from Extramarital Affairs." *Clinical Psychology: Science and Practice*, Vol. 6, 1999, pp. 382–399.

Gordon, K.C., D.H. Baucom, and D. K. Snyder. "An Integrative Intervention for Promoting Recovery from Extramarital Affairs," *Journal of Marital and Family Therapy*, Vol. 30, 2004, pp. 1–12.

Johnson, Susan M., and E. Talitman. "Predictors of Success in Emotionally Focused Marital Therapy," *Journal of Marital and Family Therapy*, Vol. 23, no. 2, 1997, pp. 135–52.

Millet, E. "The Benefit of Group Hypnotherapy in the Treatment of Sex Addictions," *Journal of Heart Centered Therapies*, 2005.

Olson, M. M., C. S. Russell, M. Higgins-Kessler, and R. B. Miller. "Emotional Processes Following Disclosure of an Extramarital Affair," *Journal of Marital Family Therapy*, Vol. 28, no. 4, 2002, pp. 423–34.

Pittman, F. S., and T. P. Wagers. "Crises of Infidelity," in N. S. Jacobson, and A. S. Gunman (eds.), *Clinical Handbook of Couple Therapy* (New York: Guilford, 1995).

Speziale, B.A. "Marital Conflict Versus Sex and Love Addiction," *Families in Society*, 1994.

Chapter 9 References

Banmen, J., and N. A. Vogel. "The Relationship between Marital Quality and Interpersonal Sexual Communication," *Family Therapy*, Vol. 12, 1985, pp. 45–58.

Buhrmester, D., W. Furman, M.T. Wittenberg, and H. T. Reis. "Five Domains of Interpersonal Competence in Peer Relationships," *Journal of Personality and Social Psychology*, Vol. 55, 1988, pp. 991–1008.

Buss, D.M., and T.K. Shackelford. "From Vigilance to Violence: Mate Retention Tactics in Married Couples," *Journal of Personality and Social Psychology*, Vol. 72, 1997, pp. 346–361.

Dutton, D. G., and A. P. Aron. "Some Evidence for Heightened Sexual Attraction Under Conditions of High Anxiety," *Journal of Personality and Social Psychology*, Vol. 30, 1974, pp. 510–517.

Fenigstein, A., and R. Peltz. "Distress over the Infidelity of a Child's Spouse: A Crucial Test of Evolutionary and Socialization Hypotheses," *Personal Relationships*, Vol. 9, 2002, pp. 301–12.

Foster, C. A., and W. K. Campbell. "The Adversity of Secret Relationships," *Personal Relationships*, Vol. 12, no. 1, 2005, 125–43.

Gottman, J.M. "The Roles of Conflict Engagement, Escalation or Avoidance in Marital Interaction: A Longitudinal View of Five Types of Couples," *Journal of Consulting and Clinical Psychology*, Vol. 6, 1993, pp. 6–15.

Gottman, J. M. "A Theory of Marital Dissolution and Stability," *Journal of Family Psychology*, Vol. 7, no. 1, 1993, pp. 57–75.

Gottman, J. M. *What Predicts Divorce: The Relationship Between Marital Process and Marital Outcomes* (Mahwah, NJ: Lawrence Erlbaum Associates, Inc., 1994).

Gottman, J.M. "Psychology and the Study of Marital Processes," *Annual Review of Psychology*, Vol. 49, 1998, pp. 169–197.

Peterson, C. D., D. H. Baucom, M. J. Elliott, and P. A. Farr. "The Relationship Between Sex Role Identity and Marital Adjustment," *Sex Roles: A Journal of Research*, Vol. 21, 1989, pp. 775–787.

Rauer, A. J., and B.L. Volling. "The Role of Husbands' and Wives' Emotional Expressivity in the Marital Relationship," *Sex Roles: A Journal of Research*, 2005.

Rusbult, C. E., and P. A. M. Van Lange. "Interdependence, Interaction, and Relationships," *Annual Review of Psychology*, Vol. 54, 2003, pp. 351–375.

Schmitt, D. P., and D. M. Buss. "Mate Attraction and Competitor Derogation: Context Effects on Perceived Effectiveness," *Journal of Personality and Social Psychology*, Vol. 70, 1996, pp. 1185–1204.

Schmitt, D.P., and D.M. Buss. "Human Mate Poaching: Tactics and Temptations for Infiltrating Existing Relationships," *Journal of Personality and Social Psychology*, Vol. 80, 2001, pp. 894–917.

Schmitt, D. P., and T. K. Shackelford. "Nifty Ways To Leave Your Lover: The Tactics People Use to Entice and Disguise the Process of Human Mate Poaching," *Personality and Social Psychology Bulletin*, Vol. 29, 2003, pp. 1018–35.

Sinclair, S.L., and G. Monk. "Moving Beyond the Blame Game: Toward a Discursive Approach to Negotiating Conflict Within Couple Relationships," *Journal of Marital and Family Therapy*, 2004.

Steuber, K. R. "Adult Attachment, Conflict Style, and Relationship Satisfaction: A Comprehensive Model," Unpublished Masters Thesis, University of Delaware, Newark, Delaware, 2005.

White, G. W., S. Fishbein, and Rutstein. "Passionate Love and Misattribution of Arousal," *Journal of Personality and Social Psychology*, Vol. 41, 1981, pp. 56–62.

Chapter 10 References

Afifi, W., W. Falato, and J. Weiner, J. "Identity Concerns Following A Severe Relational Transgression: The Role of Discovery Method for the Relational Outcomes of Infidelity," *Journal of Social and Personal Relationships*, Vol. 18, no. 2, 2001, pp. 291–308.

Brinig, M. F., and D. A. Allen. "'These Boots Are Made for Walking': Why Most Divorce Filers Are Women," *American Law and Economics Review*, Vol. 2, no. 1, 2000, pp. 126–69.

Bohannan, Paul. *Divorce and After: An Analysis of the Emotional and Social Problems of Divorce* (Garden City, NY: Anchor, 1970).

Gager, C.T., and L. Sanchez. "Two As One? Couples' Perceptions of Time Spent Together, Marital Quality, and the Risk of Divorce," *Journal of Family Issues*, Vol. 24, no. 1, 2003, pp. 21–50.

Gee, C. B., R. L. Scott, A. M. Castellani, and J. V. Cordova. "Predicting Two-Year Marital Satisfaction from Partners' Discussion of Their

Marriage Checkup," *Journal of Marital and Family Therapy*, Vol. 4, 2002, pp. 399–407.

Gordon, C. K., and D. H. Baucom. "A Multitheoretical Intervention for Promoting Recovery from Extramarital Affairs," *Clinical Psychology: Science and Practice*, Vol. 6, 1999, pp. 382–299.

Hall, J.H., and F.D. Fincham. "Relationship Dissolution Following Infidelity," in M. Fine, and J. Harvey (eds.), *Handbook of Divorce and Relationship Dissolution* (Mahwah, NJ: Erlbaum Associates, Inc., 2006).

Hargrave, T. D., and J. N. Sells. "The Development of a Forgiveness Scale," *Journal of Marital and Family Therapy*, Vol. 23, 1997, pp. 41–62.

Johnson, M.P., J. P. Caughlin, and T. L. Huston. "The Tripartite Nature of Marital Commitment: Personal, Moral and Structural Reasons to Stay Married," *Journal of Marriage and the Family*, Vol. 61, 1999, pp. 160–177.

Mongeau, P., and B. Schulz. "What He Doesn't Know Won't Hurt Him (Or Me): Verbal Responses and Attributions Following Sexual Infidelity," *Communication Reports*, Vol. 10, no. 2, 1997, pp. 143–63.

Olson, M. M., C. S. Russell, M. Higgins-Kessler, and R. B. Miller. "Emotional Processes Following Disclosure of an Extramarital Affair," *Journal of Marital and Family Therapy*, Vol. 28, 2002, pp. 423–34.

Peterson, P. R. "A Re-Evaluation of the Economic Consequences of Divorce," *American Sociological Review*, Vol. 61, 1996, pp. 528–536.

Vaughan, D. "Uncoupling: The Social Construction of Divorce," in B. Byers (ed.), *Readings in Social Psychology: Perspective and Method* (Boston, MA: Allyn and Bacon, 1993).

Waite, L.J., D. Browning, W.J. Doherty, M. Gallagher, Y. Luo, and S. M. Stanley. *Does Divorce Make People Happy? Findings from a Study of Unhappy Marriages* (Institute for American Values, New York).

Chapter 11 References

Allport, G. W., and J. M. Ross. "Personal Religious Orientation and Prejudice," *Journal of Personality and Social Psychology*, Vol. 5, 1967, pp. 432–43.

Baldacchino, D., and P. Draper. "Spiritual Coping Strategies: A Review of the Nursing Literature," *Journal of Advanced Nursing*, Vol. 34, 2001, pp. 833–41.

Diener, E., E. Suh, and S. Oishi. "Recent Findings on Subjective Well-Being," *Indian Journal of Clinical Psychology*, Vol. 24, 1997, pp. 25–41.

Enns, M.W., and B.J. Cox. "Psychosocial and Clinical Predictors of Symptom Persistence vs. Remission in Major Depressive Disorder," *Canadian Journal of Psychiatry*, Vol. 50, no. 12, 2005, pp. 769–777.

Graham, S., S. Furr, C. Flowers, and M. T. Burke. "Religion and Spirituality in Coping with Stress," *Counseling and Values*, Vol. 46, 2001, pp. 2–13.

Lazarus, R. S., and S. Folkman. *Stress, Appraisal and Coping* (New York: Springer, 1984).

Pargament, Kenneth, I. *The Psychology of Religion and Coping: Theory, Research, Practice* (New York: Guilford, 1997).

Pennebaker, J.W. "Writing About Emotional Experiences As a Therapeutic Process," *Psychological Science*, Vol. 8, 1997, pp. 162–66.

Pennebaker, J.W. and J. Seagal. "Forming a Story: The Health Benefits of Narrative," *Journal of Clinical Psychology*, Vol. 55, 1999, pp. 1243–54.

Sandllow, A. "Adaptation to Stress and Natural Therapies," *The Pain Practitioner*, Vol. 10. no. 3, 2001, pp. 10–11.

Selye, H. "A Syndrome Produced by Diverse Nocuous Agents," *Nature*, Vol. 138, 1936, p. 32.

Chapter 12 References

Barber, L., J. Maltby, and A. Macaskill. "Angry Memories and Thoughts of Revenge: The Relationship Between Forgiveness and Anger Rumination," *Personality and Individual Differences*, Vol. 39, 2005, pp. 253–262. Retrieved 21 April 2006, from: *www.le.ac.uk/psychology/jm148/paidlb2005.pdf*.

Bierman, A., E. M. Fazio, and M. A. Milkie. "A Multifaceted Approach to the Mental Health Advantage of the Married: Assessing How Explanations Vary by Outcome Measure and Unmarried Group," *Journal of Family Issues*, Vol. 27, no. 4, 2006, pp. 554–582.

Butler, M. H., S. K. Dahlin, and S. T. Fife. "'Languaging Factors Affecting Clients' Acceptance of Forgiveness Intervention in Marital Therapy," *Journal of Marital and Family Therapy*, Vol. 28, 2002, pp. 285–298.

Fincham, F.D., J.H. Hall, and S.R.H. Beach. "'Til lack of forgiveness doth us part': Forgiveness in Marriage," in E.L. Worthington, Jr (ed.), *Handbook of Forgiveness* (New York: Brunner-Routledge, 2005).

Fincham, F. D. "The Kiss of Porcupines: From Attributing Responsibility to Forgiving," *Personal Relationships*, Vol. 7, 2000, pp. 1–23.

Gordon, K. C., and D. H. Baucom. "Understanding Betrayals in Marriage: A Synthesized Model of Forgiveness," *Family Process,* Vol. 37, no. 4, 1998, pp. 425–49.

Gordon, K.C., D. H. Baucom, and D.K. Snyder. "An Integrative Intervention for Promoting Recovery from Extramarital Affairs," *Journal of Marital and Family Therapy*, Vol. 30, 2004, pp. 213–32.

Hall, J.H., and F.D. Fincham. "Relationship Dissolution Following Infidelity," in M. A. Fine, and J. H. Harvey (eds), *Handbook of Divorce and Relationship Dissolution* (Mahwah, NJ: Lawrence Erlbaum Associates, Inc., 2006).

Lloyd, Carol. "I Want You So Bad," *Salon.com*, 26 Aug. 2006.

McCullough, M. E., C. G. Bellah, S. D. Kilpatrick, and J. L. Johnson. "Vengefulness: Relationships with Forgiveness, Rumination, Well-Being, and the Big Five," *Personality and Social Psychology Bulletin*, Vol. 27, 2001, pp. 601–10.

Sprecher, S., D. Felmlee, M. Schmeeckle, and X. Shu. "No Breakup Occurs on an Island: Social Networks and Relationship Dissolution," in M. A. Fine, and J. H. Harvey (eds.), *Handbook of Divorce and Relationship Dissolution* (Mahwah, NJ: Lawrence Erlbaum & Associates, Inc., 2006).

Chapter 13 References

Bankruptcy case: *Osborne v. Stage* (In re Stage), 321 B.R. 486, 492–93 (B.A.P. 8th Cir. 2005).

Dorf, Michael C. "Should the Law Punish Adultery?" Special to *CNN.com*, 18 August 2005.

Hawley, David. "Lindy Still Flying High," 12 June 2005, *Pioneer Press, TwinCities.com.*

In re Proceeding of John A. v. Bridget M., 16 A.D.3rd 324 (1st Dept., 2005): *www.shanahanlaw.com/Marks-Decision.pdf*

Turley, Jonathan. "Of Lust and the Law," *Washington Post*, 5 September 2004, p. B01.

United States v. Angel M. Orellana, Corporal (E-4), U.S. Marine Corps, NMCCA 200201634, Decided, 29 November 2005: *www.jag. navy.mil/NMCCA/200201634.pub.doc.*

Chapter 14 References

Bachand, L. L., and S. L. Caron. "Ties That Bind: A Qualitative Study of Happy Long-Term Marriages," *Contemporary Family Therapy*, Vol. 23, 2001, pp. 105–21.

Branden, N. "A Vision of Romantic Love," in R. J. Sternberg, and M. L. Barnes (eds.), *The Psychology of Love* (New Haven, CT: Yale University Press, 1988).

Fincham, F. D., and S. R. H. Beach. "Relationship Satisfaction," in D. Perlman, and A. Vangelisti (eds.), *The Cambridge Handbook of Personal Relationships* (New York: Cambridge University Press, 2006).

Gable, S. L., H. T. Reis, E. A. Impett, and E. R. Asher. "What Do You Do When Things Go Right? The Intrapersonal and Interpersonal Benefits of Sharing Positive Events," *Journal of Personality and Social Psychology*, Vol. 87, 2004, 228–245.

Karney, B.R., and T.N. Bradbury. "Neuroticism, Marital Interaction, and Trajectory of Marital Satisfaction," *Journal of Personality and Social Psychology*, Vol. 72, 1997, pp. 1075–1092.

Kaslow, F., and J. A. Robinson. "Long-Term Satisfying Marriages: Perceptions of Contributing Factors," *The American Journal of Family Therapy*, Vol. 24, no. 2, 1996, pp. 153–170.

Knee, C. "Implicit Theories of Relationships: Assessment and Prediction of Romantic Relationship Initiation, Coping, and Longevity," *Journal of Personality & Social Psychology*, Vol. 74, no. 2, 1998, pp. 360–70.

Levinger, G., and A.C. Levinger. "Winds of Time And Place: How Context Has Affected a 50-Year Marriage," *Personal Relationships*, Vol. 10, 2003, pp. 285–306.

Mackey, R. and B. A. O'Brien. "Adaptation in Lasting Marriages," *Families in Society: The Journal of Contemporary Human Services*, Vol. 80, 1999, pp. 587–96.

O'Rourke, N., and P. Cappeliez. "Intra-Couple Variability in Marital Aggrandizement: Idealization and Satisfaction within Enduring Relationships," *Current Research In Social Psychology*, Vol. 8, no. 15, 2003.

Rauer, A.J., and B.L. Volling. "The Role of Husbands' and Wives' Emotional Expressivity in the Marital Relationship," *Sex Roles*, Vol. 52, Nos. 9/10, 2005, pp. 577–587.

Ripley, J. S., E. L. Worthington, D. Bromley, and S. Kemper. "Covenantal and Contractual Values in Marriage: Marital Values Orientation Toward Wedlock or Self-Actualization (Marital VOWS) Scale," *Personal Relationships*, Vol. 12, no. 3, 2005, pp. 317–36.

Shumway, S. T., and R. S. Wampler. "A Behaviorally Focused Measure for Relationships: The Couple Behavior Report (CBR)," *The American Journal of Family Therapy*, Vol. 30, 2002, pp. 311–321.

Sprecher, S. "'I Love You More Today Than Yesterday': Romantic Partners' Perceptions of Changes in Love and Related Affect Over Time," *Journal of Personality and Social Psychology*, Vol. 76, no. 1, 1999.

Strom, B. "Communicator Virtue and Its Relation to Marriage Quality," *Journal of Family Communication*, Vol. 3, no. 1, 2003, pp. 21–40.

Weigel, D.J., and D. S. Ballard-Reisch. "All Marriages Are Not Maintained Equally: Marital Type, Marital Quality, and the Use of Maintenance Behaviors," *Personal Relationships*, Vol. 6, 1999, pp. 289–301.

White, C. H. "Welsh Widows' Descriptions of Their Relationships: Themes of Relational Experience in Long-Term Marriage," *Communication Studies*, 2004.

Resources

Chapter 1 Resources

American Association of Sex Educators, Counselors, and Therapists (AASECT): P.O. Box 1960, Ashland, Virginia 23005-1960; Phone: (804) 752-0026, Fax: (804) 752-0056: *www.aasect.org*

American Board of Sexology: 3203 Lawton Road, Suite 170, Orlando FL 32803; Phone: (407) 574-5708 or Fax (407) 574-8943: *www.sexologist.org*

Better Sex: *www.bettersex.com*

Cleveland Clinic: *www.clevelandclinicmeded.com*

Kinsey Institute, Morrison 313, Indiana University, Bloomington, IN 47405; Phone: (812) 855-7686: *www.indiana.edu/~kinsey*

"Love Lab" information (from Dr. John M. Gottman's Web site): *www.gottman.com/research/family*

PREPARE-ENRICH Program/testing Web site operated by Life Innovations (David H. Olson, Ph.D., President): *www.prepare-enrich.com/indexm.cfm*

Processes of Adaptation in Intimate Relationships (PAIR) Project (includes the PAIR test to assess a couple's emotional, social, sexual, intellectual, and recreational intimacy): *www.utexas.edu/research/pair/ourresearch/index.html*

Chapter 2 Resources

Domestic Violence Lethality Assessment Tools by Neil Websdale, Ph.D., posted on Violence Against Women (VAW) site: *www.vawnet.org*

Frankl, Victor, E. *Man's Search for Meaning: An Introduction to Logotherapy* (New York: Washington Square Press, 1963).

Gaudette, Pat. *Midnight Confessions: True Stories of Adultery* (Lecanto, FL: Home & Leisure Publishing, Inc., 2005).

Male Menopause: *menalive.com/menowhat.htm*

National Domestic Violence Hotline: *www.ndvh.org*

Chapter 3 Resources

Gochros, Jean Schaar. *When Husbands Come Out of the Closet* (New York: Haworth Press, 1989).

How to Cheat on Your Wife (read it at your own risk): *www.cheatmanual.com/Manual%20Free%20Copy.pdf*

How Philanderers Keep Secrets: *www.philanderers.com/page_1.htm*

Leonard Lopate Show, 25 January 2006: *www.wnyc.org/shows/lopate/episodes/01252006*

Mistress Web Site: *www.heloise.co.uk/mistress.htm*

Making Love, motion picture, 1982, Director: Arthur Hiller

Nicolazzo, Janet. "The Other Side of the Closet After Ten Years and Two Children, My Husband Told Me He Is Gay," *Salon.com*, 26 April 2000.

Straight Spouse Network (SSN): *www.straightspouse.com*

Chapter 4 Resources

Antisocial Personality Disorder site, Mayo Clinic: *www.mayoclinic .com/health/antisocial-personality-disorder/AN00703*

Borderline Personality Disorder site, Mayo Clinic: *www.mayoclinic .com/health/borderline-personality-disorder/DS00442*

Borderline Personality Disorder: Raising Questions, Finding Answers (National Institute of Mental Health, NIMH): *www.nimh.nih.gov/ publicat/bpd.cfm*

Borderline Personality Disorder Today site: *www.borderlinepersonality today.com/main/*

Narcissistic Personality site, Mayo Clinic: *www.mayoclinic.com/health/ narcissistic-personality-disorder/DS00652*

Personality Disorder site, MedlinePlus (gathered from the National Library of Medicine (NLM), the National Institutes of Health (NIH), and other government agencies and health-related organizations): *www.nlm.nih.gov/medlineplus/personalitydisorders.html*

Other Woman, The (TOW) Web site: *www.gloryb.com*

Chapter 5 Resources

Cybersex Addiction Web site: *www.netaddiction.com/cybersexual_ addiction.htm*

Pro Family Web site (sponsored by the School of Family Life at Brigham Young University): *www.foreverfamilies.net*

Manning, Jill C., testimony about Internet pornography and its effects on marriage and the family, before the Civil Rights and Property Rights Committee on Judiciary United States Senate. November 10, 2005. Retrieved 2 May 2006, from: *http://new.heritage.org/Research/Family/ loader.cfm?url=/commonspot/security/getfile.cfm&PageID=85273*

Pro Marriage Web site: *www.marriage-relationships.com*

Surviving Infidelity Web site: *www.survivinginfidelity.com*

Chapter 6 Resources

Behavioral Information Site: *www.behavenet.com*

Dependent Personality Disorder Information: *www.nlm.nih.gov/ medlineplus/ency/article/000941.htm*

DSM-IV(tm) Explained: *www.psychnet-uk.com/dsm_iv/_misc/dsm_ diagnosis.htm*

eHarmony Marriage Web site: *www.eharmony.com*

Personality Disorder Web site: *www.psychiatric-disorders.com/personality/ index.php*

Personality Project Site: *www.personality-project.org*

Personality Test Sites: *www.humanmetrics.com/cgi-win/JTypes2.asp* and *www.ptypes.com/temperament_test.html* and *4np.net/ddli/*

Chapter 7 Resources

Better Sex Web site: *www.bettersex.com/compinfo/companyinfo.asp*

Christian Sex Book Web site: *www.christian-sex.net/order_risk_free_ ssch.htm*

Etcoff, Nancy, *Survival of the Prettiest: The Science of Beauty* (London, UK: Abacus Books, 2000).

Kinsey Institute Web site: *www.kinseyinstitute.org/resources/FAQ.html# fantasy*

Victoria's Secret Web site: *www.victoriassecret.com*

Chapter 8 Resources

American Association for Marriage and Family Therapy (AAMFT); 112 S. Alfred St., Alexandria, VA 22314; Phone: 703-253-0461; Fax: 703-253-0462: *www.aamft.org*

Brown, Emily M. *Patterns of Infidelity and Their Treatment* (New York: Brunner/Mazel, 1991).

EFT resource page maintained by Richard Niolon, Ph.D.: *www .psychpage.com/family/library/eft.html*

Elisabeth Kübler-Ross Web site: *www.elisabethkublerross.com*

Lusterman, Don-David. *Infidelity: A Survival Guide* (Oakland, CA: New Harbinger, 1998).

Moultrup, D.J. *Husbands, Wives, and Lovers* (New York: Guilford Press, 1990).

Pittman, Frank. *Private Lies: Infidelity and the Betrayal of Intimacy.* (New York: Norton, 1989).

Chapter 9 Resources

Buss, David M. *The Evolution of Desire: Strategies of Human Mating* (New York, NY: Basic Books, 2003).

Fisher, Helen. *Why We Love: The Nature and Chemistry of Romantic Love* (New York: Henry Holt and Company, 2004).

Gottman, J.M., *Why Marriages Succeed or Fail* (New York: Simon and Schuster, 1994).

Chapter 10 Resources

American Bar Association Family Law site at: *www.abanet.org*

Browne, Marlene. *Boomer's Guide to Divorce: And a New Life* (Indianapolis, IN: Alpha Books, 2004).

Divorce Process: *www.divorceprocess.com*

Equality in Marriage Institute sponsored by Lorna Jorgenson Wendt at: *www.equalityinmarriage.org/wd.html*

Glass, Shirley J., and Jean Coppock Staeheli. *Not Just Friends: Rebuilding Trust and Recovering Your Sanity After Infidelity* (New York: Simon and Schuster, 2003).

Moultrup, David, J. *Husbands, Wives and Lovers: The Emotional System of the Extramarital Affair* (New York: Guilford Press, 1990).

National Marriage Project, The; Rutgers, The State University of New Jersey, 54 Joyce Kilmer Avenue, Lucy Stone Hall B217, Piscataway, NJ 08854-8045; Phone: (732) 445-7922; *marriage@rci.rutgers.edu; http://marriage .rutgers.edu*

Ornish, Dean. *Love & Survival: The Scientific Basis for the Healing Power of Intimacy* (New York: HarperCollins Publishers, 1998).

Healing with Sexual Relationships (an alternative Web site filled with interesting articles with scientific information and promoting an orgasm-free sex life as a means of retaining intimacy and union, sidestepping the biochemical ups and downs associated with orgasm-induced dopamine rushes): *www.reuniting.info*

Chapter 11 Resources

Anne Morrow Lindbergh story: *www.npr.org/templates/story/story. php?storyId=5232208*

Lindbergh, Anne Morrow, *Gift from the Sea* (New York, NY: Random House, Pantheon 50th Anniversary Reissue, 2005).

Medline Plus Stress: *www.nlm.nih.gov/medlineplus/stress.html*

Multidimensional Measurement of Religiousness/Spirituality for Use in Health Research: A Report of the Fetzer Institute (National Institute on Aging Working Group, 2003). Retrieved 17 April 2006, from: *www .seminare-ps.net/Rel-Psy/Fetzer_Multidimens_Measurement_Religious-ness.pdf*

National Institute of Mental Health: *www.nimh.nih.gov/publicat/ anxiety.cfm*

Pat Gaudette's Divorce/Adultery Support Web sites: *http://divorce support.about.com*

Pennebaker, James W., Web site: *http://homepage.psy.utexas.edu/home page/faculty/pennebaker/Home2000/JWPhome.htm*

Pennebaker, James W. *Writing to Heal: A Guided Journal for Recovering from Trauma and Emotional Upheaval* (Oakland, CA: New Harbinger Press, 2004).

Selye, Hans. *The Stress of Life* (New York: McGrawHill, 1956, Rev. ed. 1976).

Selye, Hans. *Stress Without Distress* (New York: Lippencott, 1974).

Stress/Hormone Cycle: *www.drugabuse.gov/NIDA_Notes/NNVol14N1/Stress.html*

Stress Management: *www.cdc.gov/nasd/docs/d001201-d001300/d001245/d001245.html*

Chapter 12 Resources

Dickey, Christopher. *Summer of Deliverance: A Memoir of Father and Son* (New York, NY: Simon & Schuster, 1998).

Forgiving Web Site, home to Everett Worthington's Campaign for Forgiveness Research: *www.forgiving.org/default.asp*

Surviving Infidelity Web site: *www.survivinginfidelity.com*

The Smoking Gun, legal Web site where you can type a name, and find the filed pleading in the lawsuits in which they've been involved: *www.thesmokinggun.com*

Vaughan, Diane. *Uncoupling: Turning Points in Intimate Relationships* (New York: Oxford University Press, 1986).

Chapter 13 Resources

Electronic communications case, *O'Brien v. O'Brien* (Florida 5th District Court of Appeals, February 11, 2005): *www.5dca.org/Opinions/Opin2005/020705/5D03-3484.pdf*

Kelly, John F. "Virginia Adultery Case Roils Divorce Industry," 1 December 2003, *Washington Post*, p. B01. Retrieved 28 April 2006, from: *www.sodomylaws.org/usa/virginia/vanews123.htm*

Kuralt Estate v. Patricia Shannon: *www.lawlibrary.state.mt.us/dscgi/admin.py/Get/File-20803/02-348.wp9.pdf*

Manual For Courts-Martial United States (2005 Edition): *www.apd.army.mil/pdffiles/mcm.pdf*

Schorr, Daniel. "Adultery by Military Officers: A Serious Matter?" NPR archives. 14 August 2005. Retrieved 28 April 2006, from: *www.npr.org/templates/story/story.php?storyId=4799716*

Chapter 14 Resources

Branden, Nathaniel, Ph.D. Web site: *www.nathanielbranden.com*

Fitzpatrick, Mary Anne. *Between Husbands and Wives: Communication in Marriage* (London, UK: Sage Publications, 1988).

"How to Stay Married," 11 December 2003, *The Independent* via *The Age online*. Retrieved 4 May 2006, from: *www.theage.com.au/articles/2003/12/10/1070732278068.html*

Klagsbrun, Francine. *Married People: Staying Together in the Age of Divorce* (Toronto, CA: Bantam Books, 1985).

Mackey, R. A., and B. A. O'Brien, *Lasting Marriages: Men and Women Growing Together* (Westport, CT: Praeger, 1995).

Wallerstein, Judith S., and Sandra Blakeslee, *The Good Marriage: How and Why Love Lasts* (Boston, MA: Houghton Mifflin Company, 1995).

Index